May–Aug [illegible]

Day by Day with God

Rooting women's lives in the Bible

BRF
Ministries

BRF Ministries
15 The Chambers, Vineyard
Abingdon OX14 3FE
+44 (0)1865 319700 | brf.org.uk

Bible Reading Fellowship is a charity (233280)
and company limited by guarantee (301324),
registered in England and Wales

EU Authorised Representative: Easy Access System Europe –
Mustamäe tee 50, 10621 Tallinn, Estonia, **gpsr.requests@easproject.com**

ISBN 978 1 80039 502 2

Distributed in Australia by:
MediaCom Education Inc, PO Box 610, Unley, SA 5061
Tel: 1 800 811 311 | admin@mediacom.org.au

Distributed in New Zealand by:
Scripture Union Wholesale, PO Box 760, Wellington
Tel: 04 385 0421 | suwholesale@clear.net.nz

Acknowledgements
Scripture quotations marked with the following abbreviations are taken from the version shown. Where no abbreviation is given, the quotation is taken from the same version as the headline reference. NIV: The Holy Bible, New International Version (Anglicised edition) copyright © 1979, 1984, 2011 by Biblica. Used by permission of Hodder & Stoughton Publishers, a Hachette UK company. All rights reserved. 'NIV' is a registered trademark of Biblica. UK trademark number 1448790. NLT: The Holy Bible, New Living Translation, copyright © 1996, 2004, 2015 by Tyndale House Foundation. Used by permission of Tyndale House Publishers, Inc., Carol Stream, Illinois 60188. All rights reserved. NRSV: The New Revised Standard Version Updated Edition. Copyright © 2021 National Council of Churches of Christ in the United States of America. Used by permission. All rights reserved worldwide. MSG: *The Message*, copyright © 1993, 1994, 1995, 1996, 2000, 2001, 2002 by Eugene H. Peterson. Used by permission of NavPress. All rights reserved. Represented by Tyndale House Publishers, Inc. ESV: The Holy Bible, English Standard Version, published by HarperCollins Publishers, © 2001 Crossway Bibles, a division of Good News Publishers. Used by permission. All rights reserved. KJV: The Authorised Version of the Bible (The King James Bible), the rights in which are vested in the Crown, are reproduced by permission of the Crown's Patentee, Cambridge University Press. TLV: Tree of Life (TLV) Translation of the Bible. Copyright © 2015 by The Messianic Jewish Family Bible Society.

A catalogue record for this book is available from the British Library

Printed and bound by Zenith Media NP4 0DQ

Day by Day with God

Edited by **Jackie Harris** May–August 2026

Writers in this issue

Lyndall Bywater lives in Canterbury and works with The Salvation Army and Canterbury Diocese, helping people pray. She is the author of two books, both published by BRF Ministries: *Faith in the Making* and *Prayer in the Making*.

Elaine Storkey is an academic, author, broadcaster, and senior member of Newnham College, Cambridge. A former president of Tearfund, she also directed the London Institute for Contemporary Christianity for ten years and has taught in universities in the UK and overseas.

Anne Le Tissier is an author, preacher, and conference speaker, called to disciple others in their ongoing walk with God. She has been writing for *Day by Day with God* since 2005. Connect with her at **anneletissier.com**.

Jen Baker is a speaker, author, and mentor. Her mission is to see a global movement of Christian women living with courageous faith and creating kingdom impact.

Bridget Plass is a writer and speaker, appearing and touring with her husband Adrian all over the world. For the past ten years she has enjoyed being actively involved in the programme at Scargill House in Yorkshire and absolutely loves living near Durham.

Sheila Jacobs is a writer, freelance editor, and award-winning author. She is also a speaker and leads writing and contemplative retreats. She is passionate about helping others meet with Jesus and encouraging new writers. Connect with her at **sheila-jacobs.co.uk**.

Chine McDonald is a writer, broadcaster, and director of the religious think tank Theos. A regular contributor to BBC religion and ethics programmes, she is also vice-chair of Greenbelt Festival and a trustee of Christian Aid.

Jenny Sanders is an international speaker, prophetic teacher, and writer. She has been discipling and training Jesus-lovers across streams and denominations for more than 30 years. She loves helping people grasp the magnificence of God's grace and the excitement of living with him at the helm.

Sara Batts-Neale is a priest in the diocese of Chelmsford. She is currently the Anglican chaplain to the University of Essex. Married to Tim, they live with a dog and host a cat.

Catherine Larner is a freelance writer, editor, and presenter who reports on literature, culture, and faith for national, regional, and Christian magazines and local radio.

Welcome

I'm not sure who first coined the phrase 'Life's a marathon, not a sprint', but the apostle Paul said much the same thing in his letter to the Hebrews. He describes a 'race marked out for us' (12:1, NIV) which will require perseverance and keeping our eyes fixed on Jesus.

My predecessor Jill Rattle referenced this passage in her last editorial and wrote about team races, where one runner, after completing her lap, passes on the baton to the next team member. As Jill introduced me as the new editor, she wrote: 'Jackie is going to run a strong lap until it is her turn to pass the baton on again.' I remember reading that with both a sense of excitement and responsibility.

I have loved being part of the team who produce *Day by Day with God*, but I believe God is leading me to focus on other responsibilities, so now it's my turn to hand on the editorial baton and to cheer on Becca Turnbull, who is busy working on the September–December issue. Becca is part of the content creation team at BRF Ministries, so is already familiar with the notes and excited to take them forward. I know she has some great topics planned for the next issue.

It's been such a privilege to be part of this ministry, and I am so grateful to our fantastic team of contributors who are always willing to tackle different subjects and themes, and to share their experiences and what they have learned. I have so appreciated their insights and wisdom.

I would also like to thank the readers who have contacted us with valuable feedback on the notes, and those who have recommended us to friends or have bought subscriptions to encourage others. Your support is so important and spurs us on to continue inspiring women to root their lives in the Bible.

These notes have been a huge blessing to me in many ways – I have learned a lot, made new friends, and experienced God ministering to me through them. They have encouraged me in the race marked out for me, and I'm praying that they will continue to bless and inspire you in your spiritual journey.

'May the grace of the Lord Jesus Christ, and the love of God, and the fellowship of the Holy Spirit be with you all' (2 Corinthians 13:14).

Jackie

Jackie Harris, Editor

Songs of Ascent

Lyndall Bywater writes...

Welcome to the May–August edition of *Day by Day with God*, where we begin our Bible studies in the book of Psalms. For the next 16 days, we will be reading through a rather special section of the psalms, known as the Songs of Ascent.

These songs probably weren't all written at the same time or by the same person, but gradually, over the centuries, they were gathered into a little song cycle which the people of Israel would sing as they made their way from their homes to Jerusalem for the annual festivals. These were songs of worship, but they were also journey songs, sung to help keep up morale on the long and often arduous climb to the holy city.

I live in Canterbury, where we are familiar with pilgrimage. Not only does our cathedral commemorate the martyred Archbishop Thomas Beckett, but the city was also the inspiration for the 14th-century author Geoffrey Chaucer's *Canterbury Tales*.

The premise of Chaucer's tales is that a group of pilgrims are challenged to a story-telling competition, and so each has to think of one or two stories which might entertain his or her companions so successfully that they win a prize. Sadly, Chaucer never got to finish the work, so we don't know who won. The tales we do have are funny, scandalous, and profound in equal measure, and they reveal a lot about pilgrims. Even when the object of their journey is to encounter God in a holy place, pilgrims still bring all their humanness with them: their quarrels and conflicts, their pride in themselves and in those they love, and their collective wisdom about life.

While the Songs of Ascent are a long way from a Chaucer tale, they too contain wonderful glimpses into the humanness of the pilgrims on that road to Jerusalem. We will find songs about spouses and children; songs about the history they're so proud of, and the enemies they're so angry with; songs about the beauty of Jerusalem and the goodness of God. These psalms prove again what I love so much about the Bible – that God is in the mundane and the everyday as much as the dramatic and the spectacular.

As you make these readings part of your own pilgrimage from Easter to Pentecost, may they help you to find God in every part of your life.

Getting going

I am for peace; but when I speak, they are for war. (v. 7, NIV)

Imagine you're sitting in your armchair, enjoying the comfort and tranquillity of a moment's rest. What is it that's most likely to get you moving? Will it be the prospect of a good cup of tea or the conviction that you've sat still long enough and there are jobs to do? Much as I recognise the call of the kettle or the chiding of a chore unfinished, I confess that, at my time of life, it's most likely to be the grumbling of my bladder that gets me on my feet. Sometimes discomfort is the only thing that motivates us to move.

Psalms 120—134 are called the Songs of Ascent, and they most likely acquired that name because they were the psalms which the people of Israel would recite as they made their way from their hometowns to Jerusalem for one of the annual religious festivals. They were psalms of movement – songs to sing as the people walked up the steep hills to Jerusalem – and they would most likely sing them in the order in which we find them in our Bibles today.

This first song is an interesting place to start. We might reasonably expect a cheerful ditty about hitting the road or heading off on an adventure, but instead we find a lyrical grumble about how bad things have got at home. The psalm mentions Meshek and Kedar, places a long way from Jerusalem, and the psalmist is thoroughly disgruntled with the lying and warmongering going on around him. It's as though he's telling his fellow travellers, 'I just had to get out of there!'

In truth, perhaps that's where a lot of movement begins. We get so tired of the way things are that we just have to get up and get going, in search of something better.

Is there some discomfort or frustration that's stirring you to move? Is God allowing you to see how bad things have got, so you can get up and follow the leading of the Spirit to a new and better place?

LYNDALL BYWATER

Getting orientated

I lift up my eyes to the mountains – where does my help come from? My help comes from the Lord, the Maker of heaven and earth. He will not let your foot slip – he who watches over you will not slumber. (vv. 1–3, NIV)

Mountain climbing isn't for the faint-hearted, and neither is it for the ill-prepared. Mountain rescue teams often comment on the fact that the people they go to help simply haven't got the right kit with them. Among the most important things to have with you are appropriate orientation tools, a map and compass, and sturdy footwear – shoes that will support your feet and stop you from sliding.

That's the vision this psalm conjures up for me, as I picture family groups from all over Israel and Judah setting out to make the steep climb to Jerusalem. Hiking boots and GPS wouldn't be around for millennia, but they knew the importance of stable footing and sound orienteering. This Song of Ascent would remind them to lift their eyes to the mountains, keeping their focus on the place they were heading and to put their trust in God, the one who would keep their feet from slipping.

We never walk alone. Whether we're travelling from the old to the new, whether we're going in the right or the wrong direction, whether we're alone or en masse, our loving Father, who neither slumbers nor sleeps, always has his attention on us. It's easy to slip into a 'reward and punishment' theology which suggests that when we're getting it right, God looks out for us, and when we're going astray, God ignores us, but that isn't what the Bible says. This psalm is only eight verses long, yet five times it tells us that God watches over us. God's eyes are on us in our comings and goings, no matter where we're coming from or going to.

Have you ended up somewhere you never meant to be? Take heart! God is still watching over you and God will help you find the right road again.

Father God, I seem to have got myself a bit lost. I've ended up somewhere I didn't want to be. Thank you for watching over me. Would you take my hand and lead me to where I need to be? Amen.

LYNDALL BYWATER

Getting away

I was glad when they said to me, 'Let us go to the house of the Lord.' And now here we are, standing inside your gates, O Jerusalem. (vv. 1–2, NLT)

For nine years, I organised the prayer venue for The Salvation Army's ROOTS Conference, where thousands of people from all over the country gathered for a weekend of worship, teaching, and seaside fish and chips. We would set up a huge marquee full of prayer stations, then have the privilege of seeing hundreds of people use the space as a place to meet with God. It became the high point of my year, and I can still remember the excitement I felt as I made that train journey from Canterbury to Southport, full of anticipation at what God would do during the weekend. I truly was glad!

Big festivals have been around for a long time. The Songs of Ascent are the story of God's people at the high point of their year, making their way to a festival, and this psalm brims over with the excitement of that prospect. Not only are they heading to a wonderful event, but they're also heading to a wonderful city. They sing about Jerusalem, its architecture and its history, its fortifications and its wealth. One thing's for sure, it's nothing like where they come from; somehow that's important.

Thanks to the internet, we can now join in with almost anything at almost any time. We no longer need to make the journey to spectacular places, because we can hover over them with a mouse from the comfort of our own homes. Even so, we were created for connection and fellowship. We may not be called to make pilgrimage to Jerusalem, but it does us good to step out of what we are familiar with and take ourselves to places which strike awe into us and to journey with others who are as thirsty for an encounter with God as we are.

Is there anything which you would describe as a spiritual high point of your year? Are there moments in your life when you feel that sense of anticipation about going somewhere or gathering with God's people?

LYNDALL BYWATER

Receiving mercy

As the eyes of servants look to the hand of their master, as the eyes of a maid to the hand of her mistress, so our eyes look to the Lord our God, until he has mercy upon us. (v. 2, NRSV)

I am blind, and when I received my current guide dog, I had to learn a new way of training her. The Guide Dog Association has adopted what is known as positive reinforcement training, a method by which the dog receives a food reward for each bit of work it does. As my dog Venus performs the various tasks of guiding me safely, I hand her pieces of kibble. Being a Labrador, she loves this, and it keeps her attention firmly riveted on me in general and on my hand in particular.

Today's reading is another Song of Ascent which would have been sung as the people of Israel made their way up to Jerusalem for one of the annual festivals. As songs so often do, these psalms tend to have a line or keyword which is repeated several times, and today the keywords are 'eyes' and 'hand'. The writer of this song is imagining their eyes fixed on the hand of God. Unlike my dog Venus, though, they aren't looking for treats.

This song is a cry for mercy. It mentions slavery and servitude, contempt and scorn. It's the song of a people who feel overlooked and downtrodden, yet who are trying hard to keep their eyes fixed on the hand of the one who is their true master, the one who can give them all they need. They sing to remind one another that theirs is the God of mercy.

Just a few weeks ago, we were remembering Jesus' hands, stretched out on a cross and scarred for love of all humankind. As we navigate the complexities of a world where things aren't as fair and just as we'd like them to be, let's keep our eyes fixed on those hands, where there is always mercy and grace in abundance.

Jesus Christ, your hands healed the sick and raised the dead. Your hands held little children and washed feet. Your loving hands were crushed and pierced for me. Help me never lose sight of the hands that make me whole. Amen.

LYNDALL BYWATER

Receiving freedom

We escaped like a bird from a hunter's trap. The trap is broken, and we are free! Our help is from the Lord, who made heaven and earth. (vv. 7–8, NLT)

How quickly do you get into the holiday mood? Are you the sort of person who's ensconced on the sun lounger within minutes of turning on your 'Out of office' notification or are you more the sort of person who takes a few days to really believe you're free from the duties and demands of work?

When the people of Israel made their journey to Jerusalem, it was a holiday. There would be religious observances, of course, but mostly there would be family, friends, and feasting. Today's Song of Ascent has something of a holiday feel to it. There is joy and relief at being free from past troubles and deep gratitude to the God who has made things turn out right in the end, but there are some deeper layers to this song.

Four of the Songs of Ascent are credited to King David, and this is one of them. If anyone is qualified to talk about being helped to conquer his foes and being rescued from traps, it's David. His entire reign was spent dealing with Israel's enemies and establishing peace in the land. There was rarely a time he wasn't being pursued, attacked, or plotted against by someone somewhere.

These days we are rightly reticent to claim God as being 'on our side,' but for David, who faced the threat of death daily, those words were nothing less than heartfelt testimony. He knew God as the one who had set him free, and he left his people a song to remind them of the fact.

You and I have the same story to tell. We may not have faced Bronze Age warriors, but we have wrestled with sins and fears, temptations and addictions, and God, through Jesus Christ, has set us free from every trap and every foe.

Freedom is ours, but much like holidays, it can take us a long time to settle into it. Is there an area of your life where God has promised you freedom but you're struggling to accept it and live in light of it?

LYNDALL BYWATER

Receiving reassurance

Those who trust in the Lord are like Mount Zion, which cannot be shaken but endures forever. As the mountains surround Jerusalem, so the Lord surrounds his people both now and forevermore. (vv. 1–2, NIV)

I went to Israel several years ago, and our itinerary included visiting the River Jordan, then getting into our coach and driving up to Jerusalem. The journey is only about 20 miles, but the Jordan is several hundred metres below sea level, whereas Jerusalem is almost 800 metres above sea level. In just 20 miles, you climb almost 1,200 metres (equivalent to three quarters of a mile).

Not only did that short journey make my ears pop a lot, but it also gave me a sense of what the journey to Jerusalem would have been like for those who travelled to the annual festivals from lowland areas. Given the steepness of the climb, I'm guessing some of these Songs of Ascent would have been sung in a rather breathless manner. I'm also guessing that the idea of mountains would have become very concrete to them as they trudged up. There were mountains all around them, even under their feet.

While mountains may be tough to climb, they are fantastic defences for a city. If you're surrounded by them, it's very difficult for your enemies to attack you, and that's exactly why the psalmist is encouraging those pilgrims to look up and be grateful for the very topology which is making their legs ache. Those mountains are to remind them of the strength and protection of the God they worship.

Another pilgrim who may well have made that climb, the apostle Paul, wrote that God's eternal power and divine nature can be understood and seen through the things God has made (Romans 1:20). When we want to remind ourselves of who God is, we do well to look at the beauty of the natural world. When we need reassurance in the most uncertain of times, we do well to muse on a mountain.

As spring brings life to our gardens and green spaces, why not take some time to look for God's fingerprints in nature. What aspects of God's character do you notice? Where do you see power? Where do you find love?

LYNDALL BYWATER

Sowing tears

Those who sow with tears will reap with songs of joy. Those who go out weeping, carrying seed to sow, will return with songs of joy, carrying sheaves with them. (vv. 5–6, NIV)

I remember once hearing an old fable about a woman who had two buckets, one perfect and the other cracked. She would put them on the ends of a pole across her shoulders and carry them to the nearby stream. The perfect one would carry a full load of water home, whereas the cracked one would leak water out along the way. One day someone mocked her for using a broken bucket. Pointing to a host of flowers growing along the side of the path where the leaky bucket had passed, she said: 'I know my bucket leaks. That's why I have been planting seeds.'

I would definitely have tried to fix the bucket rather than plant seeds, but sometimes our longing to fix things causes us to miss the beautiful possibilities that come with brokenness.

Today we find our pilgrims climbing to Jerusalem with a song of two halves in their mouths. The first half is an exuberant reminiscing about all the amazing things they've experienced in the past, but the second half takes a sadder turn. Things aren't so good now, and they're not afraid to include that truth in their singing together.

As is often the way with the psalms, the final verses bring hope in the midst of hardship. They bring resolution, but it's important to notice that they don't bring a solution. They don't offer ways to fix the problems. Instead, they call to mind the God-given processes of planting and watering, sowing and growing.

I grew up in a culture where we thought problems should get fixed and tears should be dried, yet it's as though the psalmist is saying: 'Don't worry about fixing or hiding. Just keep walking and let the tears fall. You never know what new life might spring from them.'

Loving God, I want answers, solutions, and fixes. You want faith, growth and new life. Today I choose to trust you in the unresolved, and to allow my tears to flow, that beautiful things might spring up along the way.

LYNDALL BYWATER

Weeding out comparison

Unless the Lord builds a house, the work of the builders is wasted. Unless the Lord protects a city, guarding it with sentries will do no good. (v. 1, NLT)

I don't usually watch daytime television, but I was keeping my dad company in hospital recently and found myself watching the quiz show *Jeopardy*. If you've never seen it, it involves contestants being given a word or phrase which is the answer to a question, and their job is to work out what the question would be.

I'm reminded of this as I ponder these Songs of Ascent. If the pilgrims to Jerusalem struck up one of these psalms, would it have been in response to a specific conversation they were having, and if so, what were they talking about, for that particular song to come to mind?

There's a specific scene I see in my mind when I think of why someone might come to Psalm 127. I imagine people who have got to that stage in a relationship where they start sharing their achievements: conscientious men talking about building homes for their wives; diligent soldiers talking about how well they perform their duties; and proud parents telling anyone who'll listen just how well their children are doing. And since these pilgrims are all too human, maybe a bit of one-upmanship is creeping in.

Today's psalm is the ultimate leveller. An ancient poem of King Solomon, it reminds everyone, singers and listeners alike, that everything we have comes from God. We bring our gifts and talents, but it's God who guides and empowers our work; it's even God who gives us rest. It's God who keeps us safe and it's God who entrusts our children to us. It's so easy to start comparing ourselves to one another, when the truth is that we all stand equal before God – equally seen, equally valued, and equally loved.

Loving God, forgive us when we compare ourselves to others, needing to prove ourselves better. Teach us to enjoy what we have, to care for what we hold, and to do our best in the things you've called us to. Amen.

LYNDALL BYWATER

Harvesting blessing

You will enjoy the fruit of your labour. How joyful and prosperous you will be! Your wife will be like a fruitful grapevine, flourishing within your home. Your children will be like vigorous young olive trees as they sit around your table. (vv. 2–3, NLT)

I've been involved with the 24–7 Prayer movement for many years now, and like all movements, it has developed its own language – words and phrases which seem to capture its DNA. One of those phrases is, 'Pray your best prayer.' That doesn't mean pray a prayer that is theologically impressive or anything like that. It means to think of the best things you can imagine God doing for anyone, then instead of asking God to do those things for you, you ask God to do them for someone else.

Yesterday we reflected on our need to be reminded that everything we have comes from God, particularly when we are tempted to compare ourselves to others or boast about our achievements. Today we arrive at Psalm 128, and discover we've moved another step further on. Now we're not just counting our blessings and thanking God. This time we're focusing our attention on someone else other than ourselves. Suddenly we're not saying 'we' anymore; we're saying 'you'. This isn't a song about our lives, our journeys, our wants and needs; this is a prayer for someone else. Indeed, it's not just a prayer, it's a generously lavish blessing. The person singing this song really is praying their best prayer for that other person.

This kind of prayer has power. It's not wishful thinking. Throughout the Old Testament, we read of God teaching the people to memorise prayers of blessing, to speak blessing over each other, to be a blessing to the world around them. Blessing is God's own language, and when we bless others, God joins in. We pray our best prayer, thinking up the very best blessings we can imagine for the person we're praying for, and God delights to back our meagre words with acts of love and power.

Who has God put on your heart today? Why not spend some time composing your very best prayer for them: a prayer of blessing which sets out all the things you long to see come to fulfilment in their life.

LYNDALL BYWATER

Refusing bitterness

May all who hate Jerusalem be turned back in shameful defeat... And may those who pass by refuse to give them this blessing: 'The Lord bless you; we bless you in the Lord's name.' (vv. 5, 8, NLT)

Research shows that groups become more generous to each other the longer they are stuck in an unideal situation together. When we board a train, we tend not to give much thought to our fellow passengers. We keep to ourselves. But fast-forward to a moment when that train has got stranded somewhere, and we passengers become far more generous, offering our snacks around, using our phones to get information for each other and helping entertain each other's bored children. Adversity tends to breed solidarity.

The tenth Song of Ascent begins with solidarity: an invitation to everyone to join in. However, this is no happy sing-along. This is a collective cry of pain, with its graphic description of physical violence. There's no doubt that pouring out our pain and distress together is cathartic, but do you notice what happens next? The pain turns to bitterness and hatred towards anyone who is outside of that experience, or who might see things differently.

The culmination of this chorus of defiance is a blatant refusal to bless. We noted yesterday how powerful blessing is – how it is God's native language – and that makes this withholding of blessing all the more severe.

The reaction is entirely understandable. Why wouldn't we reject anyone who causes us pain? Why wouldn't we protect ourselves by cutting them off? Yet Jesus, who literally carried those scars on his back so vividly described in verse 3, chose the way of blessing, and if we follow him, we too need to choose that way.

Let's return to our train carriage, where solidarity has turned to collective anger towards the train crew. When the guard walks through that door, will you and I be the ones who still speak blessing, no matter how frustrated and disappointed we may feel?

Blessing isn't the same as forgiveness, and I often find I can bless even when I'm not ready to forgive. Is there someone you're struggling to forgive? Why not try handing them to God and praying God's blessing over them.

LYNDALL BYWATER

Waiting intentionally

I wait for the Lord, my whole being waits, and in his word I put my hope. I wait for the Lord more than watchmen wait for the morning, more than watchmen wait for the morning. (vv. 5–6, NIV)

I live in Canterbury, and when I visit our famous cathedral, I always feel moved by the way the steps inside the building are worn away. Each one has been smoothed and shaped by the feet of the millions of people who have made pilgrimage to that place over the past eight centuries or so. But it's not just feet that have trodden the stone, it's knees too. It was tradition that, if they were able, pilgrims would make the last part of their journey on their knees, as a sign of their humility before God.

Journeys often sharpen our focus. Today's Song of Ascent finds the Israelites continuing to climb up the steep road to Jerusalem, travelling in community on a journey which would have taken most of them several days at least. Some of them wouldn't have seen each other for months, so there would've been plenty of catching up, celebrating, and commiserating with one another, not to mention having a grumble about life's injustices. However, with this song the focus shifts and for the rest of the song cycle, their focus is Jerusalem and the God who calls that city home. Perhaps that's not surprising, given that the only way to meet with God was to go to where God lived.

What of us today? We live in the glorious light of Pentecost, the Spirit of God with us at every moment of every day yet somehow hunger for God still matters. We don't have to make pilgrimage to find God, but we do still need to hunger and to seek. It's as though God's presence can only truly be experienced, by us and by those around us, when God's people humbly continue to long for it with all our heart.

If God is present, always close, always with us, what might it mean for us to wait for the Lord with our whole being? Are there practices you can build into your daily routine to help you wait for God?

LYNDALL BYWATER

Cultivating calm

But I have calmed and quieted my soul, like a weaned child with its mother; my soul is like the weaned child that is with me. (v. 2, NRSV)

Have you ever tried to help a toddler calm themselves down? It's not an easy task. First there are all the exciting things that need looking at and asking about. Then there's the obligatory dancing, the wild animal impressions, and the impromptu handstands that can't possibly wait until another day. And then, when they do finally sit down on your knee, the calm lasts all of 20 seconds before life's next great adventure sweeps them away again.

Yesterday we were talking about the way our focus sharpens as we get nearer to the end of a journey; the way we see more clearly and hunger more deeply. Today's Song of Ascent has a similar theme. The psalmist is reflecting on letting go of burdens, anxieties, and distractions so they can find a place of peace in God. He likens his soul to a weaned child. In the culture of the time, a weaned child would have been a toddler. Do you ever feel like you have a 'toddler soul'? I'd say mine has distinctly toddler tendencies when I sit down and try to focus on God in prayer. I'm ever amazed at the random topics that flit through my brain, not to mention the sudden desire to get up and do something – if not a handstand, then the hoovering instead.

If you've ever cared for a toddler, you'll know that the best thing you can do is to keep drawing them back to you, lovingly and gently, till their brains slow down enough to be at peace. I wonder if prayer is similar: the tender process of drawing our souls gently back into the quiet place; not reprimanding ourselves for failing but lovingly bringing our wandering souls back to the embrace of God, who loves us more than we know.

Loving God, I give thanks for the gift of a soul so full of energy, so stirred by wonder. Help me to love my 'toddler soul' as much as you do and help me to find calm in your presence. Amen.

LYNDALL BYWATER

Supernatural presence

We heard that the Ark was in Ephrathah; then we found it in the distant countryside of Jaar. Let us go to the sanctuary of the Lord; let us worship at the footstool of his throne. (vv. 6–7, NLT)

I am part of a prayer community in Canterbury, and the place where we meet has been a place of prayer for about 940 years. I was telling an American friend this fact the other day, and his gasp of astonishment reminded me of how fortunate we are to have such deep wells of prayer in the place where I live. The place where we pray truly is a 'thin place', where the presence of God is somehow more tangible.

I wonder if that was part of the excitement of going up to Jerusalem. The temple was the place where the ark of the covenant had finally found its permanent home, and the ark was a precious and highly spiritual artefact which the people of Israel understood as signifying the very presence of God.

With the ark of the covenant, we circle back round to thinking about the presence of God, as we were on Monday. The ark isn't part of our Christian worship tradition, because we know that God, through his Son, has poured his Spirit over all humankind, no longer to be contained in one place. Through his Spirit, we now have the church – that diverse and glorious collection of human beings who carry the presence of God in our very lives.

Verse six of today's psalm is a reminder that the ark had a chequered history. It had been captured and moved, housed in the temples of foreign Gods and even in someone's home, and everywhere it had been, things had happened. Everywhere it had rested, things had changed for the better.

It's a challenging thought that we, in some way, might be the new ark. When we land somewhere – when the church takes up residence in a community – do things change for the better?

Pray today for the church congregations in your local community, that they will be beacons of hope and refuges of love and kindness; that every believer will be a sower of blessing and a carrier of God's life-changing presence.

LYNDALL BYWATER

Natural niggles

**'I will live here, for this is the home I desired. I will bless this city and make it prosperous; I will satisfy its poor with food. I will clothe its priests with godliness; its faithful servants will sing for joy.'
(vv. 14–16, NLT)**

I sat on a bench in the garden of Gethsemane on a warm day in early November. What an experience, to be so close to where Jesus had prayed on the night before his crucifixion. I expected something profound and powerful, but as I stilled myself to soak in the atmosphere of the place, all I could hear was rush-hour traffic, and all I could feel were the mosquito bites on my feet.

Our pilgrims are very nearly at Jerusalem now, and for some it will be their first ever visit. When I read these verses towards the end of Psalm 132, I imagine a young person singing them; someone who's never seen Jerusalem before, but who is caught up in the wonder of these words. Soon they're going to set foot in the city God calls home. And then I imagine an older person walking next to them, who knows all about the noise, the smell, and the busyness of a big city, praying that the young person won't be disappointed if the place isn't all they thought it might be; praying that the humanness of the place won't stop them sensing the presence of God.

When I was in Gethsemane, I had to screen out the niggles and distractions to connect with the presence of God in that place, and that reminds me of what it's like when I gather with other Christians for worship. God promises to dwell with any group of believers who gather in Jesus' name (Matthew 18:20), and perfection isn't required. That means God dwells amid our imperfections, our failings, and our frustrating habits. We too can learn to bear with what is imperfect, that we might encounter the one who is goodness itself.

Is it difficult to worship with your Christian family at the moment? Why not imagine Jesus sitting next to you in church. Talk to him about the things making you sad or angry and see what he says.

LYNDALL BYWATER

Together in unity

How wonderful, how beautiful, when brothers and sisters get along! It's like costly anointing oil flowing down head and beard... It's like the dew on Mount Hermon flowing down the slopes of Zion. Yes, that's where God commands the blessing, ordains eternal life. (vv. 1, 3, MSG)

The story is told of two mice who found a morsel of cheese on the pantry shelf. Such was their determination not to let the other mouse get it that they fought over it, and such was the intensity of their tug-of-war that they entirely failed to notice the huge piece of cheese sitting just above their heads... until a rat popped its head up and whisked it away.

The people of Israel lived in tribes and clans. Descended from the patriarchs and bound by a common faith, there was much to unite them, but we all know what tribes and clans are like, and these tribes skirmished with each other over land, crops, wells, marriages, property, and anything else they felt the need to defend or contest.

Nevertheless, here they are, all climbing up to Jerusalem, all singing their way through the same cycle of songs, and today's song is about unity. I wonder if there's a reason why this song comes so late in the cycle. Perhaps it would have been a difficult one to sing at the start of the journey, when those tribal squabbles felt very real and very important. Yet, as the land falls away behind them and home becomes a distant memory, as the city of God looms large and they prepare to mingle with thousands of others from different corners of that same great family, perhaps unity becomes more possible.

What about us, the church? Are we ever in danger of missing out on the delicious big chunk of cheese because we've got stuck squabbling over the little things? Can we turn our steps towards the new Jerusalem, turn our faces towards Jesus, and let the oil of God's presence soak us until we really do behave like one big, loving family?

Today the Novena begins, the nine days of prayer between Ascension and Pentecost. As we remember the first disciples praying together in that upper room, waiting for the Spirit, let's pray for the unity of the church in our day.

LYNDALL BYWATER

Everyday worship

Praise the Lord, all you servants of the Lord who minister by night in the house of the Lord. Lift up your hands in the sanctuary and praise the Lord. May the Lord bless you from Zion, he who is the Maker of heaven and earth. (vv. 1–3, NIV)

Weary after a long day of touring in the hot sun, we sat down, each of us making ourselves as comfortable as we could on one of the ancient steps. Someone started singing, and we sang out prayers of blessing over the city of Jerusalem. The sound was beautiful. It will be one of my lasting memories.

The steps in question belonged to a flight which would once have led up to the ancient temple, and I think of them again as we reach the end of our Songs of Ascent. Not only would these psalms have been sung on the road to Jerusalem, but they would also have been sung as the pilgrims made their slow way up those steps to the temple – one psalm for each step.

And perhaps it is that slow walk into the temple which explains something about today's reading. After all the anticipation, you might imagine this final song would be an explosion of awe-struck praise, but it's not. It's a short, humble ode to the people on the nightshift. The temple may be the very seat of God's presence on earth, but, like everything else in this world, it runs on the faithful commitment of people turning up to do their jobs, at all hours of day and night.

As I sat on those temple steps, singing my heart out, I was deeply aware of being one voice among millions who have sung in that place over the millennia, and I was filled with hope. No matter how dark our world gets, how contested the city of Jerusalem may be, how difficult things get in our own lives, the people of God keep singing. We keep ministering for God, day and night, and God, who made heaven and earth, will bring all things to fulfilment.

God of our hours and our years, our daytimes and our night-times, help us to keep singing. Whether the praise feels glorious or the song is more of a beleaguered croak, help us to keep on worshipping you. Amen.

LYNDALL BYWATER

The person and work of the Holy Spirit

Elaine Storkey writes…

People often contrast the portrayals of God in the Old and New Testaments and feel uneasy at differences. 'Why,' I was once asked in a lecture, 'is God presented as a singular divinity in the Old Testament without reference to Jesus and the Holy Spirit, whereas in the New Testament God has a multiple personhood – Father, Son and Spirit?'

The answer is quite simple. That's not the Old Testament presentation of God! Even though it's a common misunderstanding, it was rejected long ago by the earliest theologians, many of whom saw the Trinity revealed in the Hebrew scriptures. Thinkers like Origen and Irenaeus point not only to the Messianic references to Jesus, but also believe he appears in the Old Testament in pre-incarnational form (e.g. Genesis 16:7; 22:11–12).

However, if this requires a bit of thought, seeing the Holy Spirit in the Old Testament doesn't. The many explicit references made to the Spirit's work and divine power make the evidence compelling. The first mention is in the very second verse of the Bible (Genesis 1:2) and references occur right through to the final chapter of Revelation.

The Holy Spirit is there at the beginning, in the very act of creating the world. The Spirit is also the one who speaks through the prophets, challenging and rebuking evil and calling people to repent. The Spirit warns of captivity and desolation and graphically describes destruction and loss. The Spirit reminds people of God's covenant, brings God's promise of restoration, and leads captives into freedom. The Spirit also directs the prophets in foretelling the coming of the Messiah, identifying his sufferings and his ultimate triumph. Joel even predicts the Day of Pentecost, when ordinary people will be overwhelmed with the Spirit's power.

The Spirit of God in the Hebrew scriptures is the same Holy Spirit of the New Testament. In the gospels, Acts, and the epistles, the Holy Spirit continues the work of enlightening, convicting, consoling, and empowering. Working with the Father and Son, the Spirit endures throughout history, opening the hearts of millions of human lives to God's love and saving power. You and I can be thankful today that God's Spirit continues to breathe life and truth into our broken world, and impart truth, wisdom and courage to those who stand faithfully for Christ.

The Holy Spirit active in creation

In the beginning God created the heavens and the earth. Now the earth was formless and empty, darkness was over the surface of the deep, and the Spirit of God was hovering over the waters. (vv. 1–2, NIV)

This image of the darkness and emptiness of precreation, where water is part of the nothingness of form or being, is stark. Yet already God's Spirit is hovering (or 'brooding') over the waters. The Hebrew authors choose their words carefully. The word for God's Spirit, 'breath', is one of the metaphors for the Holy Spirit in the New Testament. The word for 'brooding' is one given to birds on their eggs, waiting for new life to burst forth. So, at the very beginning of the Bible, we see God the creator preparing to breathe life into a world created from nothing. And the Holy Spirit is active in this creating process.

Christian theologians from the earliest times have also seen this as an implicit statement of God the Trinity. They see it reinforced in Genesis 1:26, where God says, 'Let us make mankind in our image', and in Genesis 3:22, where after humans first sin God says, 'The man has now become like one of us, knowing good and evil.' In these references to plurality, we get glimpses already of the Father, Son, and Spirit that we see in the New Testament. Our language for God will always be inadequate; calling God 'Trinity' is the best we can do to make sense of what the Bible reveals. Yet many Christians find it tallies also with their own different experiences of the way they relate to God.

The Holy Spirit as co-creator didn't stop at the creation but has been evident throughout history. Through the Holy Spirit at work in prayerful humans, we see creative results in wonderful music, art, science, cultivation, architecture, medicine and so much else. I've even known the Spirit's leading in the ordinary tasks of every day. Perhaps you have also.

Are there times in your life when you have been aware of the Holy Spirit's help in undertaking commitments or projects? Are there times now, when you might especially need that help?

ELAINE STORKEY

The Spirit speaks into leadership

'The Spirit of the Lord spoke through me; his word was on my tongue. The God of Israel spoke, the Rock of Israel said to me: "When one rules over people in righteousness, when he rules in the fear of God, he is like the light of morning at sunrise."' (vv. 2–4, NIV)

The prophet Samuel believes these final words of King David on leadership are given to him by God's Spirit. David, the youngest son of Jesse, descendant of Ruth and slayer of the giant Goliath, was probably the most important king of Judah and Israel. The Holy Spirit had already spoken through King David as he wrote many of the psalms. So, what is the Holy Spirit teaching us here?

First, that godly leadership must always be exercised with justice. God is the God of justice who holds rulers to account and requires them to rule in the 'fear of God' (v. 3). Second, that just rulers bring blessings on themselves and others: they're likened to the sun rising on a morning without clouds and new grass springing up after rain. It's a picture of peace and freedom where people can flourish without conflict. Third, even though rulers fail, God is faithful. God made a covenant with David, despite the many things that David did wrong.

That's an understatement; in many ways David's reign was a disaster. He endured a civil war and years of famine. He sent Uriah the Hittite to his death when Uriah's wife, Bathsheba, became pregnant with David's child. He underwent recurring family crises, including an attempted coup from his son. Yet David's remorse and trust in God brought forgiveness and meant that his reign was blessed and celebrated through history. It would be from David's line that Jesus was born, whose utterly just and blameless rule is the measure for all leaders.

In these days, when rulers are self-serving and truth is at a premium, we need spiritual discernment to know what to believe and whom to trust. The Holy Spirit still speaks through sinful human beings, both in churches and nations, but true repentance and faith are needed first.

Lord, we pray that you will raise up godly leaders who will rule the nations of the world with justice and neighbourly love, and that you will remove those who cause harm and destruction. Amen.

ELAINE STORKEY

The Spirit gives wisdom and revelation to the prophets

The Spirit of the Lord will rest on him – the Spirit of wisdom and of understanding, the Spirit of counsel and of might, the Spirit of the knowledge and fear of the Lord. (v. 2, NIV)

How do we know if the Holy Spirit is speaking? Sometimes churches can discern the Spirit's voice, but not always. When the Hebrew prophets addressed the people, it was clear that God's Spirit was speaking wisdom through the prophet. Often God was rebuking the people for abandoning their faith, as when the Spirit entered Ezekiel and gave him words of 'lament and mourning and woe' (Ezekiel 2:10) to the rebellious nation. Isaiah has also just been warning people of God's impending judgement on Israel, but now the Holy Spirit is directing him to a new theme – the coming Messiah.

The Spirit affirms that a Messianic leader from David's line ('the stump of Jesse') will bring people to salvation. He will be imbued with the Spirit's power and full of wisdom and understanding. Wisdom directs his counsel and righteousness steers his judgements. Nothing about this leader is superficial. The Spirit gives Isaiah a glimpse of the reign of peace to be ushered in when people accept this Messiah. The wolf and lamb live together, and a young child plays near cobras and vipers without harm. It sounds like a new Eden, with wars forgotten and creation restored.

Christians have always accepted that this passage refers to Jesus and that Isaiah's prophecy points subtly to the intertwining of Father, Son, and Spirit. Is that what Isaiah intended? We don't know, and it doesn't matter. What we do know is that the Holy Spirit gave the prophet the inspiration and wisdom to see God's crucial vision for the world we live in. Despite its advanced technology and AI, our world seems very short on wisdom. Maybe Christians need to listen more to the Spirit of God, to bring deeper wisdom and discernment to our own age.

In Isaiah 58, the people of God are clearly out of step with the Spirit of God. Can you list the things they are getting wrong, and what that says to us today?

ELAINE STORKEY

The Spirit foretells the Messiah

The Spirit of the Sovereign Lord is on me, because the Lord has anointed me to proclaim good news to the poor. He has sent me to bind up the broken-hearted, to proclaim freedom for the captives. (v. 1, NIV)

I love the way the Spirit speaks through Isaiah in this powerful Messianic prophecy. The intimacy between the Spirit and the Anointed One shows their unity in bringing encouragement, healing, freedom, and deliverance to those who badly need it. Every detail seems sensitively in touch with our human predicament. Good news for the poor, freedom for captives, and restoration of sight are deep reassurances. Those subject to grief or despair will have their spirits raised; those in bondage will find liberation. The wonderful picture of replacement – beauty for ashes, gladness for mourning, praise instead of despair – all come through this godly leader in the Spirit's power.

So, it's no surprise to find Jesus in a synagogue, unrolling the scroll at this prophecy (Luke 4:14–20), for he's the one appointed by the Father and anointed by the Spirit to bring about these changes in people's lives. Isaiah was prophesying to the people of Israel that God would restore their brokenness, but he was also looking into the distant future when people would find restoration in Jesus. Throughout his earthly ministry, Jesus brought new life and new hope to those who had hit rock bottom.

The Holy Spirit's ministry doesn't end with the New Testament. Right down the ages and across the globe today, the Spirit of God is still active in lives, communities, and nations. Whatever you face today, you can ask the Holy Spirit to stay close and be your guide. Whether today brings joy or difficulties, God has not forgotten your needs. When we reach out to Jesus, each of us can know that the Spirit of the Sovereign Lord is here for us too.

Where might you need the Holy Spirit's help today? Are there other people you know who also need that help? As you reflect on the compassion of our Messiah, pray that today will be marked by love and care.

ELAINE STORKEY

The Spirit poured out on believers

'And afterwards, I will pour out my Spirit on all people. Your sons and daughters will prophesy, your old men will dream dreams, your young men will see visions. Even on my servants, both men and women, I will pour out my Spirit in those days.' (vv. 28–29, NIV)

The Holy Spirit has just used Joel to warn the people, giving them the picture of a plague of hungry locusts devouring and destroying everything. The metaphor then changes to that of a mighty army intent on wiping them out as the prophet calls on the people to leave their rituals to repent and return to God (2:13). The series of assurances that follow culminates in this promise of the outpouring of the Holy Spirit.

However, it must have been strange for the people to read these words from the prophet. They were used to God communicating his words of truth and prophecy through key leaders of Israel, most of them men rather than women. Religious status and public esteem were important. Yet here Joel foretells a new future, where the Holy Spirit shows that God is no respecter of human status. People without connections or credentials, money, or influence will all be candidates for receiving empowerment and blessings as the Holy Spirit is poured out.

The church received this outpouring at Pentecost, but it hasn't stopped there. Through the ages the Holy Spirit has led young and old, women and men, servants and lords into spiritual leadership. The outpouring is not always noisy and strident, however. Gifts from the Spirit are just as likely to be those of gentle discernment and quiet teaching, given not to elevate the speaker but to bless the church.

Has your church accepted the inclusiveness and breadth of the Spirit's gifting? If human beings decide to overrule the Holy Spirit in deciding who has gifts that may be exercised or which are of greater value, we can miss the outpouring that the Spirit has promised. And our loss is immeasurable.

Thank you, Lord, for the vision you gave Joel. Help us all to bring it alive and active in our churches today, with the guidance of your Holy Spirit. Amen.

ELAINE STORKEY

The Spirit manifesting God the Trinity

When all the people were being baptised, Jesus was baptised too. And as he was praying, heaven was opened and the Holy Spirit descended on him in bodily form like a dove. And a voice came from heaven: 'You are my Son, whom I love; with you I am well pleased.' (vv. 21–22, NIV)

Not many baptisms reach the peak of this one! It's a magnificent visual representation of the Trinity. The voice of the Father affirms his love for the Son as the Holy Spirit descends gently on Jesus in the form of a dove. I wonder if the others who were being baptised really understood what was happening – that right in front of them the Hebrew prophesies were being fulfilled and God's Spirit was descending in power on the Messiah.

At least John the Baptist knew. He was taken aback when Jesus joined those coming to be baptised in the River Jordan. Jesus did not need to be baptised; he had no sin that had to be symbolically washed away. Nevertheless, John accepted Jesus' request and witnessed the presence of God the Trinity. Why did Jesus come for baptism? Clearly he wanted to affirm the ministry of his cousin John. But I believe he also wanted to identify publicly with our humanness, and for this to become a hallmark for his time on earth.

Every baptism celebrates the Christian belief in Father, Son, and Spirit, whether through total immersion or gathered around a font. For some Christians it is also an act of bravery. Many who are persecuted for their faith must take the decision to be baptised with prayer and courage. Open Doors reported the murder of a Christian convert in Iraq who was to affirm her faith publicly by being baptised. It was on International Women's Day. Her body was found on the side of the road, tied with tape and with many stab wounds. In wanting to identify with Christ in baptism, this precious sister also identified with him in death.

Let us stay vigilant and prayerfully support organisations that protect others who want to confess belief in Father, Son, and Spirit.

Open Doors publishes its World Watch List each year to give us information about the persecuted church and encourage us to support them. Download a copy online to guide your prayers.

ELAINE STORKEY

The Spirit as our teacher and advocate

'I will ask the Father, and he will give you another advocate to help you and be with you forever – the Spirit of truth... The Holy Spirit, whom the Father will send in my name, will teach you all things.' (vv. 16–17, 26, NIV)

Promises usually don't come out of nowhere, and the promise of a new advocate for the disciples comes after several significant conversations in the upper room. Jesus has predicted that Peter will deny him, has quietly identified Judas as betrayer and told the disciples that he will be going to the Father. The disciples are understandably disturbed.

Struggling to understand, Thomas wants to know the way to the Father. Jesus replies enigmatically that he himself is the way, the truth, and the life. Philip wants to see the Father. Jesus replies that anyone who has seen him has seen the Father. The confusion and fear of the disciples is palpable. Judas has already left, unwilling to be confronted by truth.

The disciples couldn't have fully grasped the significance of Jesus' promise. He was going, but he was leaving his body behind. He had already done that symbolically in the last supper. Now, the disciples would be the body of Christ, a body which would grow and expand to the uttermost parts of the world. And the Holy Spirit would live in the body, teaching the disciples and generations to come the truths about the Father and Son and how to serve God in our own time and era. This Holy Spirit of truth, the advocate and teacher, would stay as advocate and teacher until the very end of time.

Today we are members of Christ's body and recipients of Jesus' promise. The Spirit of truth battles now against the lies of our age, especially those in high places. Living in truth matters in every area of our lives, and while holding on to truth today can be costly, it is our Christian calling.

Pilate asked: 'What is truth?' Today, when leaders lie and social media spreads rumours and untruths, it's hard to know what's true. Programmes such as More or Less *on BBC Radio 4 can help with this.*

ELAINE STORKEY

The Spirit of power and witness

'You will receive power when the Holy Spirit comes on you; and you will be my witnesses'... When the day of Pentecost came, they were all together in one place... All of them were filled with the Holy Spirit and began to speak in other tongues as the Spirit enabled them. (1:8; 2:1, 4, NIV)

Last night marked the end of the Feast of Weeks in the Jewish calendar. This event, 50 days after the Passover, traditionally celebrates both Harvest and the Torah. However, in this passage from Acts, it's turned into something totally unexpected – an outpouring of divine power and revelation on a massive scale.

Thousands of Jews had gathered in Jerusalem, with the disciples and other followers together in some large area of the temple precinct. The sound of rushing violent wind surprised them and 'tongues of fire' resting on each one must have been dramatic and overwhelming. Finding themselves speaking in languages they didn't know, the outburst of noise and talking was so animated it could be heard everywhere.

It shouldn't surprise us that the Holy Spirit chose communication as the first outworking of Pentecost. Jesus' followers might not have known the languages coming from their lips, but others did. Faithful Jews had travelled across regions to be in Jerusalem for their festival. Luke mentions places they came from and their linguistic diversity, yet through this outpouring of the Holy Spirit, God spoke to everyone in languages they knew.

The amazing, unforgettable event seems to have transformed the Jewish festival. Immediately, it gave Peter the opportunity to preach to the vast audience, desperate to know what was going on. He could remind them of Joel's prophecy, tell them about Jesus – his crucifixion and resurrection – and urge them to repent. The Holy Spirit's power to convict was evident and 3,000 people became Jesus' followers and were baptised.

As we celebrate Pentecost, let's ask the Holy Spirit for more power in our churches so we can share the gospel in ways that people understand.

Lord, please pour out your Spirit afresh on us, and give us a deeper understanding and ability to speak to others about you in words and ways that they understand. Amen.

ELAINE STORKEY

The Spirit gives hope

And hope does not put us to shame, because God's love has been poured out into our hearts through the Holy Spirit, who has been given to us… May the God of hope fill you with all joy and peace as you trust in him, so that you may overflow with hope by the power of the Holy Spirit. (5:5, 15:13, NIV)

Having the Holy Spirit in our lives doesn't inoculate us against suffering. Many strong, faithful Christians face disaster or hardship and wonder why. Unhelpful people sometimes suggest that it's because of lack of faith, but that is rarely true. In fact, Jesus predicts that his followers will have 'tribulation' because of their faith. Often suffering comes simply because of the brokenness of the world we live in. We cannot always escape the painful things that afflict others.

Yet Paul says in this passage that we can still have peace with God. He even suggests we might 'glory' in our sufferings when they produce perseverance in us and strengthen our character. Whatever the external circumstances of our lives, we can reach out for the Holy Spirit to pour love and hope into our hearts. Paul's prayer for the Christians in Rome wasn't that they would never struggle or suffer, but that the Holy Spirit would fill them with hope and peace.

During my life I have met Christians who have felt utterly defeated after too many disappointments and setbacks. One friend, drained and exhausted, said her life was 'running on empty' and confided that she had even contemplated ending it if nothing changed. In my spirit I felt that worse was yet to come for her and was very disturbed. When I shared this as gently as I could, I suggested we should pray together and ask the Holy Spirit to give her hope. Three days later she phoned me. Things had got worse, but she felt different. The Holy Spirit had lightened her heart and sustained her; she now had the hope needed to see her through.

God led that friend into blessing others through a caring ministry. The Holy Spirit can bring hope to any one of us.

Think of anyone you know who is facing desperation right now and needs the Holy Spirit to lift their spirits. Pray that God will flood their heart with hope and help them to persevere.

ELAINE STORKEY

The Spirit confirms God's salvation with miracles

This salvation, which was first announced by the Lord, was confirmed to us by those who heard him. God also testified to it by signs, wonders and various miracles, and by gifts of the Holy Spirit distributed according to his will. (vv. 3–4, NIV)

The Holy Spirit's miraculous power has always been a source of fascination. I wonder if you've had much experience of miracles. I must confess that my encounter with them is limited, and I'm particularly cautious of churches who claim miracles happen regularly. However, I have seen them on a few occasions: once when scars left by months of self-damage began to fade and disappear, and another where someone's sight was suddenly and inexplicably restored as we were praying and praising God. Experiences like this make me realise that miracles are real.

From a biblical standpoint, miracles are purposeful. They are never for entertainment value nor to bring personal adulation to the miracle-worker. 'Signs' point beyond themselves to something greater, often to God's identity and the presence of God's Spirit in the world. They are 'wonders' because of their impact on us. By their very nature miraculous events evoke amazement or awe; they open our hearts more to God.

The author of Hebrews links signs and wonders to the salvation Jesus offers; they testify to its authenticity and bear witness to the fact that the message of Jesus is far more than human wisdom, it is backed by divine power. When Jesus performs miracles, they serve as signs of his authority over the whole creation. Miracles also provide evidence of the outworking of the gospel as seen in the many signs and wonders performed by the apostles after the resurrection and ascension of Jesus (Acts 2:43; 5:12).

Yet many of us recognise the small miracles which happen in the ordinary everydayness of life. For these also show us the depths of the Holy's Spirit's love and power and help us rejoice in the gifts God gives us.

What are the miracles in your life? Why not draw up a list and thank God for each one of them.

ELAINE STORKEY

The Spirit sets us free

Therefore, there is now no condemnation for those who are in Christ Jesus, because through Christ Jesus the law of the Spirit who gives life has set you free from the law of sin and death... those who are led by the Spirit of God are the children of God. (vv. 1–2, 14, NIV)

Paul was very conscious of the Holy Spirit's power to set us free from whatever bondage holds us captive. He had been in bondage to a fanaticism which led him to persecute Christians and try to destroy the church. So, when he writes of no condemnation for those in Christ because the law of the Spirit sets us free, he's speaking from deep personal gratitude.

I suspect that Paul's division between two 'laws' rings a bell for most of us. 'The law of sin and death' means a way of life anchored in self-driven preoccupation and desire. In our contemporary world this has become normality. Self-interest underlies much motivation in personal and national life. It lies behind the disregard for other people, behind abuse, behind profiteering that drives the vulnerable into debt, and behind the pumping of sewage into our rivers.

On a global scale the law of sin and death fosters hostility between nations, where the powerful can bully the weaker and constantly threaten war with weapons of mass destruction. This law builds up separation and isolation and increases alienation from God. It's a law that, quite literally, brings death (vv. 6, 13).

We can only be set free personally from the law of sin and death by Christ and the Holy Spirit. But those who are freed can operate together under the law of the Spirit to challenge the mindset of our cultures and draw them closer to alignment with God's will. Churches can pray and work for peace, put structures in place that enable neighbourly love to thrive, and engage in reconciliation and restoration. The needs are endless and it's a big agenda, but the Spirit can lead the way, for we are the children of God.

If God stirs your heart, pray whether you should be involved in the 'big picture' and check out organisations like Open Doors, Green Christian, Restore, Christian CND, Christians in Politics, Just Love, and others.

ELAINE STORKEY

The Spirit gives spiritual gifts to the church

Now to each one the manifestation of the Spirit is given for the common good. To one there is given through the Spirit a message of wisdom, to another a message of knowledge by means of the same Spirit. (vv. 7–8, NIV)

I remember my first experience of a church singing in tongues. After a time of open prayer, someone began to sing quietly. I didn't understand the words. Then another voice came in with different words and music, blending beautifully together. Within a few minutes the whole church was singing in different tongues with such exquisite rich harmony and depth that it could have come from one of the greatest composers. When it finished, the music left us with an overwhelming sensation of God's greatness and love.

The gifts of the Holy Spirit are gifts for the church, for its edification and growth and to equip believers for service. They are not for personal glory or self-promotion but are given to strengthen the body of Christ and advance God's kingdom. Paul constantly returns to this theme of 'body', showing how spiritual gifts help each part of the body to function effectively. That is why we are given such a variety of gifts: preaching, prophecy, tongues, interpretation, faith, hospitality, administration, generosity, miracles, healing, discernment, and many more. Some of them, like gifts of healing, show tangible signs of God's active power; others, like knowledge and administration, help the church to make godly decisions and grow into maturity.

Sometimes we discover our gifts through prayer or from observations of others. I always knew I had the gift of teaching and have exercised it all my life, but I was surprised when someone told me I had the gift of discernment. Though often consulted by people for advice, I thought nothing of it. But laid before God in prayer, it became part of my calling. What gifts of the Spirit has God given to you to help build up the body of Christ? I wish you all joy in discovery.

Lord, search my heart and show me any gifts I have not yet used in my service of your kingdom. Please equip me so that I can play my part in witness and building up the church. Amen.

ELAINE STORKEY

The fruit of the Spirit in our lives together

But the fruit of the Spirit is love, joy, peace, forbearance, kindness, goodness, faithfulness, gentleness and self-control. Against such things there is no law. (vv. 22–23, NIV)

Paul has just given a formidable list of 'works of the flesh': negative behaviours and attitudes like adultery, promiscuity, idolatry, sorcery, hatred, jealousies, selfishness, envy, and a host of others. He then contrasts these with the 'fruit of the Spirit', which he commends: love, joy, peace, forbearance, kindness, goodness, faithfulness, gentleness, and self-control.

We probably all know people who exhibit some of these positive attitudes. Some of those I know are not Christians, but their temperaments are patient and gentle. I also know Christians who are irritable and low on self-control and who struggle to be patient or gentle.

Temperament, however, is not Paul's concern. He's not inviting us to pick and choose the ones that might suit our temperament better. Nor is he suggesting nice attitudes for placid people. I once read Paul's list out to a group of fairly new Christians. One man observed: 'They're not very masculine. Paul is trying to make men more like women.' Laughter led to a fascinating discussion about whether the Holy Spirit was gender-biased!

What the Spirit actually offers is a clear list, for every temperament and gender, of the fruit that God wants all Christians to grow in as a way of life. Paul uses the singular term 'fruit' to show they're a unified manifestation of life in the Spirit. Though 'spiritual' fruit, they're profoundly earthy and practical, fostering inner resilience and moral integrity. Together they encourage selflessness, empathy, harmony, and reliability; they promote care for others and trustworthiness. The fruit of the Spirit grows through prayer and effort, but it has a transformative role in all our relationships and promotes peace. As it matures, it becomes fruit which enriches those around us and helps them taste God's love.

Which aspect of the fruit of the Spirit comes most easily to you and which do you find hard to cultivate? Why? How might you develop it more? Which do you value most in your relationships?

ELAINE STORKEY

The Spirit gives wisdom and reveals God

I keep asking that the God of our Lord Jesus Christ, the glorious Father, may give you the Spirit of wisdom and revelation, so that you may know him better. I pray that the eyes of your heart be enlightened... Whoever has ears, let them hear what the Spirit says to the churches. (Ephesians 1:17–18; Revelation 3:6, NIV)

Paul's prayer for the Ephesian church was that they might know God better, but they could only do that with the Holy Spirit's help. The Spirit alone enlightens the 'eyes of our heart'. Paul's focus on the heart is a biblical one. For it is in our hearts that we make all the key decisions of life and decide on our values. While the fool says in his heart (rather than his intellect) that there is no God (Psalm 14:1), the Christian opens her heart to the prompting of the Spirit to learn more of what God wants us to know. The Holy Spirit reveals God by unveiling divine truths, guiding our hearts into a fuller understanding of Jesus and the work of his kingdom. The Spirit inspires the scriptures and affirms our identity in Christ.

I want to end our study of the Holy Spirit by looking at how he speaks to the churches. The same Spirit who 'hovered' pre-creation hovered over the churches named at the end of Bible, encouraging and rebuking. In the book of Revelation, the constant refrain is: 'Whoever has ears, let them hear what the Spirit says to the churches.' And the seven churches he speaks to desperately needed to hear the problems he identified. A decline in their first love, tolerance of false teaching, spiritual deadness, and lukewarm faith were all holding up the work of the Spirit and the spread of the gospel.

I pray that none of these are true of your church today. I don't know how much you hear the Spirit in your church, but we could all hear more if we listened better. So, let's pray together that the Holy Spirit will fall afresh on us as we worship the God of love and renew our zeal.

We pray, Father, that we will be blessed by your Holy Spirit to a greater love for you and our Saviour, and that we will be even more equipped for your service in our lives. Amen.

ELAINE STORKEY

The story of Esau

Anne Le Tissier writes…

What comes to mind when you think of Esau?

When I began writing these notes, I knew that Esau had particularly hairy skin (Genesis 25:25; 27:11). Unlike his quiet, home-loving twin brother Jacob, I recalled that Esau was rugged and adventurous, 'a man of the open country' (25:27, NIV). He was a skilled hunter, not least for the wild game (or deer) that his father so enjoyed eating (25:28; 27:3). I also knew that he fathered a nation called 'Edom', a word which can mean 'red', possibly alluding to his noticeably red skin at birth and for the red stew he bartered in exchange for his birthright (25:25, 30–33). On reflection, I realised I had quite a shallow perception of Esau based on his outward appearance, his skills, and his mistakes.

To be honest, Esau doesn't have the best reputation in scripture. At face value it appears that God hated Esau (Malachi 1:2–3). But Esau was long dead when these words were written; it was his rebellious descendants whom God had issue with. Furthermore, Paul also explains in his letter to the Romans that the 'love-hate' language was about God choosing Jacob over Esau to carry on Abraham's family line and form the nation of Israel. Admittedly, Esau isn't remembered favourably in the book of Hebrews, but we shall look at that further on Monday. So, let's have an open heart to this man, for there is more to him than these wide-sweeping statements, and there are gems to be mined from his story.

For now, in the light of my initial shallow opinion of Esau, let's take a moment together to consider how we perceive others. Do we judge them, react to them, or think we understand someone based on their outward appearance, their skills and abilities, or their reputation (i.e. by how others judge, understand, or talk about them)? It is natural for us to think we know someone from such things, but scripture is clear that God looks at the heart. Esau's heart was certainly in a sorry place at the outset of his story, but years passed in which he changed.

Whatever our story and wherever we are in our journey with God, I trust that Esau will prompt us to think on our own lives, that his mistakes might challenge us and his turn of heart encourage us.

Jostling or yielded?

The babies jostled each other within her, and she said, 'Why is this happening to me?' So she went to enquire of the Lord. (v. 22, NIV)

Some of us have been pregnant, some of us haven't, but maybe only a few of us can relate to the extreme pain that Rebekah suffered during pregnancy. She had longed for children, so she was surely elated when Isaac's prayer for her was answered. But how quickly the agony robbed her joy as the babies jostled within her, a word in Hebrew which suggests a violent struggle.

'Why is this happening to me?' she cried. Perhaps she wondered if she'd done something to deserve it, but God dismissed any such fears when he answered her anguished prayer: 'Two nations are in your womb, and two peoples from within you will be separated; one people will be stronger than the other, and the elder will serve the younger' (v. 23).

God ordained that Rebekah's younger son, Jacob, not her elder son, Esau, would continue their father and grandfather's line in fathering the nation of God's people, Israel. The prophecy was announced over two unborn babies. Neither had behaved well or badly. Neither deserved favour or reprisal. But God had already chosen his purpose for them.

We too have God-given roles, circumstances, and spiritual gifts which God planned for us before we were born (Psalm 139:16; Acts 13:36; 1 Corinthians 12:11; Ephesians 2:10). This story raises questions to prayerfully reflect on and respond to. Are we 'jostling' for another person's role or reputation? Are we embittered by someone else's ease, success, or promotion; blind to God's promises and presence with us and the potential he has equipped us to accomplish? Are we grumbling because we've not received what we or our culture believes is right, fair, or expected? And, if so, is our jostling causing pain, shame, or distress to someone else?

If something I've written now resonates, take a moment to be honest with God. Open your heart to his immeasurable love for you and his many promised blessings as you devote yourself to the roles he has ordained for you.

ANNE LE TISSIER

Contempt for God's ways

He said to Jacob, 'Quick, let me have some of that red stew! I'm famished!'... Jacob replied, 'First sell me your birthright'... So he swore an oath to him, selling his birthright to Jacob... He ate and drank, and then got up and left. So Esau despised his birthright. (vv. 30–31, 33–34, NIV)

If you were to be buried, what epitaph would you hope to be written on your tombstone? How might you wish to be described in a tribute or obituary? What words would epitomise how people remembered you? I doubt any of us would wish to be remembered as Esau is in Hebrews 12:16, for being immoral and ungodly or, as the King James translates, 'profane' – meaning he lived for worldly things. All because he 'despised' his birthright (Genesis 25:34).

Esau's craving to 'gulp some of this red stuff' (v. 30) – a more accurate translation according to one Bible commentary – demonstrates his priority for immediate satisfaction. Esau lived for worldly, tangible things no matter the cost, holding contempt for God's life and promises.

Admittedly, God had chosen Jacob over Esau to head up the wider family and lead his people, but Esau could still have chosen to love, honour, and serve God. Furthermore, Esau's contempt for something of such worth proved his innate lack of interest in God's covenant promises, which were intrinsic to a birthright inheritance. And so, having satisfied himself, he 'got up and left' (v. 34); he walked away unconcerned by his choice.

We are heirs through Christ of an eternal inheritance of life with God, including many blessings and promises to enjoy now. Consequently, Esau's story prompts us to consider if we too are turning our back on these promised blessings in our pursuit of untamed passions or distractions. Let's invite God to search our hearts for any attitude, habit, goal, or perspective that spurns his immense yet tender love for us and the beautiful, wholesome, holy, vibrant, creative life that he longs to enrich us with and that he longs for us to find fulfilment in as we devote ourselves to him.

Loving Father, please search my heart to show me if I am treating your promises flippantly or turning my back on them. Forgive my contempt for your ways. I seek to fully embrace them once again. Amen.

ANNE LE TISSIER

All were at fault

Esau said, 'Isn't he rightly named Jacob? This is the second time he has taken advantage of me: he took my birthright, and now he's taken my blessing!' Then he asked, 'Haven't you reserved any blessing for me?'... Then Esau wept aloud. (vv. 36, 38, NIV)

For 18 months I endured an unresolved problem and felt increasingly upset by the unfair treatment. Then one day in prayer I sensed the Holy Spirit convicting me of little ways I had contributed, over many years, to what was now a painful issue. Falling on my knees in confession, God's loving mercy flooded my soul.

This memory came to mind while reading today's story. Isaac was at fault for planning to give the birthright blessing to Esau, despite God's prophetic words for his sons (25:23). Esau was at fault for preparing to break his oath to Jacob (25:33), for although his outburst implied that the birthright and blessing were separate, they were in fact, intrinsically linked; the former inevitably leading to the latter. And so Esau, who had despised God's covenant, would reap the consequences of choosing his freedom to live outside the boundaries of God's blessing (27:39).

Rebekah and Jacob were also both at fault for not trusting God with his promise. Taking matters into their own hands, their scheming and deception inflicted deep pain on Esau, but also on themselves; for home-loving Jacob had to flee, separating Rebekah from her favourite son (27:42–45).

Some of you will not have contributed anything to a current problem, grievance, or hardship. You are the genuine victims of godless, vile and potentially violent behaviour. I am praying for you now. May God strengthen, support and guide you.

Others of us, however, may have blamed someone for our situation and allowed bitterness, anger, or self-justification to fill our hearts and minds, blinding us to any small part we may have contributed. Our ever-loving God waits patiently for us to discern this, confess it, receive his forgiveness, and place our hand in his once again, for whatever the future may hold.

All-loving and faithful God, thank you for this opportunity to see my heart as you do. Please convict, comfort and guide me with whatever I could say or do in the problems that I face. Amen.

ANNE LE TISSIER

Trust and forgiveness

Esau held a grudge against Jacob because of the blessing his father had given him. He said to himself, 'The days of mourning for my father are near; then I will kill my brother Jacob.' (v. 41, NIV)

I was distraught and deeply upset by someone spreading malicious slander among my friends and on social media. But as I cried out to God, his distinct response took me by surprise with words I wasn't aware came straight from scripture: 'No weapon forged against you will prevail, and you will refute every tongue that accuses you. This is the heritage of the servants of the Lord, and this is their vindication from me' (Isaiah 54:17). It was tempting to gossip, to justify myself, or even retaliate, but seeking to keep my heart tender, I trusted God with his promise, which he graciously fulfilled.

The aggrieved Esau was hurt and upset by Jacob's behaviour; that is understandable. But his desire to avenge himself by killing him conflicted with God's nature as well as his purpose for his brother. Jacob's deceitful behaviour was wrong, but it was God's role to judge and discipline him, not Esau's. Esau's reaction, however, proved once again that he trusted in himself rather than God.

We feel Esau's pain. At surface level it feels unfair. But we cannot escape Christ's call on our lives to forgive others in the same way that God forgives our many failings (Matthew 6:14–15) and to trust him with the how, where, and when he chooses to discipline those who've caused hurt and harm (Deuteronomy 32:35–36; Romans 12:19).

Offering forgiveness can be tough; it may feel almost impossible in our own strength. Our choice to trust God is a vital step, helping us to not merely speak words of forgiveness but to mean them, as God's love and forgiveness comforts, informs, and transforms our hearts.

Focus on God's love for you, his goodness and purposes. Speak out your trust in him. Then, if it helps, open your hands to symbolise your desire to let go of words or behaviour that seek self-justification or vengeance.

ANNE LE TISSIER

Unwise choices

Esau then realised how displeasing the Canaanite women were to his father Isaac; so he went to Ishmael and married Mahalath, the sister of Nebaioth and daughter of Ishmael son of Abraham, in addition to the wives he already had. (28:8–9, NIV)

Esau would have known the story well, how Grandfather Abraham had insisted his servant swear to find a wife for his son, Isaac, from their own relatives, rather than from the Canaanites (24:1–4). By accepting this principle that would later be written in Mosaic law (Deuteronomy 7:1–4), Abraham and Isaac honoured God's hand on their family and future. Sadly, however, Esau allowed his passions to guide his choice, and married two Canaanite women, who 'were a source of grief' to his parents (26:34–35).

When Jacob, however, was sent to find a wife from their own people, Esau 'realised how displeasing the Canaanite women were to his father' (28:8). Esau didn't seek God's guidance, talk it through with his parents, or urge his wives to adopt his family's faith. Instead, he acted impulsively and married an Ishmaelite (28:9). Admittedly, she was a relative, but it didn't resolve the problem with the wives he already had, and her people, like himself, did not walk with God.

Esau's rash, inconsiderate, self-motivated choices invite us to consider our own. If past choices were wrong and if they aggravated or hurt someone, do we need to ask forgiveness of God and perhaps others? Are there ways we can make amends?

As for current decisions, let's pause, pray, and perhaps ask godly, discerning friends for their counsel. Which of our options choose God's will, reflect his character, adopt his lifestyle, and align our perspective to his? Which options look to other people's needs as well as our own? How do we sense God is leading us?

When we ask for wisdom God will give it to us. 'But when [we] ask, [we] must believe and not doubt' (James 1:6). How might you trust God's response to help your choice?

Thank you, Father, for your promise to guide my choices as I seek to honour your ways and your will with my life. Please help me discern your guidance for the choices I face today. Amen.

ANNE LE TISSIER

A heart turned back to God

[Jacob] went on ahead and bowed down to the ground seven times as he approached his brother. But Esau ran to meet Jacob and embraced him; he threw his arms around his neck and kissed him. And they wept. (33:3–4, NIV)

Many years intervened between Jacob's hurried escape from Esau's wrath and his return to Canaan with wives, children, servants, and a wealth of livestock. On hearing of Esau's approach with 400 men – a sizeable fighting unit – Jacob was understandably afraid for his own and his family's safety (32:7, 11). He sent gifts to appease his brother, divided his family into groups to save some from potential massacre, then took the lead, bowing down seven times as he approached Esau, a true sign of humble submission. But 'Esau ran to meet Jacob and embraced him; he threw his arms around his neck and kissed him. And they wept' (33:4).

It is a beautiful reconciliation that brings tears to my eyes. God had worked in both men's hearts during those interim years, humbling Jacob's pride and teaching him to rely on God's promise instead of his own self efforts, while softening Esau's heart who had amassed great wealth too. In fact, we later read that Esau had named his firstborn son Eliphaz, meaning 'God is fine gold', and his second son 'Reuel', meaning 'Friend of God' (Genesis 36:4); all this is evidence of Esau's new devotion to God. Picturing Esau run to Jacob proves the full force of his love, compassion, and total forgiveness (much like the prodigal son's father in Luke 15:20).

Today's story prompts us to prayerfully consider how God might be at work in our hearts too. Are we drawing close to his love or remaining withdrawn? Are we responding to conviction or resistant? Do we thank him for his blessings or take them for granted? Are we justifying our attitudes or humbly yielding to his ways and his purposes? Just a few questions to lead us into a quiet moment of prayer.

God's love, compassion, and forgiveness are reaching out to you. Run to him as he runs to you and fall into his embrace. What do you want to say to him? Listen for his response.

ANNE LE TISSIER

Seeing the bigger picture

This is the account of the family line of Esau (that is, Edom)... This is the family line of Esau, the father of the Edomites. (vv. 1, 43, NIV)

For 150 years the fourth plinth in London's Trafalgar Square remained empty until it was topped with its first exhibit: Mark Wallinger's life-sized statue of Jesus – bound, flogged, and crowned with thorns. Wallinger called it *Ecce Homo*, 'Behold the man', echoing Pilate's response to a bawling crowd (John 19:5). But the mob, crying 'Crucify', failed to see the bigger picture of God's redemptive story unfolding through the 'man' Jesus, God's precious Son. We now see and acknowledge who he is, and I also trust that is true for how we see Esau.

Chapter 36 paints the bigger picture of Esau's life and legacy. Its broad brushstrokes remind us that his carelessness towards God and his sense of betrayal and hunger for vengeance were just chapters in that story. Esau's growing family formed a clan which grew into the nation of Edom. Sadly, in later generations, relations between Israel and Edom grew hostile, but that was their doing, not Esau's. In fact, Genesis 36 is preceded by the tender image of Esau and Jacob standing together united in grief as they buried their father, Isaac (35:28–29).

If we are stuck in past regret, distracted by busyness and overwhelm, immersed in present pleasures, or pursuing our own goals, let's turn our attention heavenwards to our true life in Christ (Colossians 3:1–3), the life that will outlive our past and present days. Scripture repeatedly urges us to choose God's life, but it's our love for him that inspires a devoted response. This week's story *was* Esau's. Christ's story was, is, and will always be. Let's keep walking in step with Jesus until we see him face-to-face, adopting his character and ways as we hold fast to his presence and promises in the ups and downs of life.

Lord Jesus Christ, I behold you. I gaze on your divine being and beauty. I worship you. Thank you that my story is now grafted into yours. Thank you for your many promised blessings for today and forever. Amen.

ANNE LE TISSIER

What it means to be heirs of Christ

Jen Baker writes...

Placing a hot cup of coffee next to me, I sat before my keyboard with a particular direction in mind – focusing on our inheritance in Christ. It wasn't long before unplanned concepts began taking shape as words rapidly filled the pages. One of the most satisfying parts of writing is seeing fresh thoughts, seemingly out of nowhere, appear on the page as you type. It's as if each click of the keyboard releases another piece of the puzzle. One theme that appeared repeatedly was the reality of our spiritual inheritance reaching far beyond our own lives.

We see this beautifully illustrated in Abraham's life and, of course, in the life of Jesus, who is the reason we have an eternal inheritance. In a world fuelled by ego and driven by money, one can be hard pressed to find individuals who are truly living a sacrificial life of obedience to their Saviour. What would that look like for us? How do we do this practically? We will explore these themes over the next few weeks, but first let's prepare our hearts to receive.

Have you ever asked the Holy Spirit to walk through every room of your house, highlighting things he wanted removed? Have you asked him what, if anything, fights for your worship? How are you ensuring your spiritual inheritance is flowing through you and not only to you?

One amazing truth is that our godly inheritance can be accessed now, not solely after death. With this in mind, we will be focusing on the benefits of inheritance – why it's important and how we can practically outwork what is rightfully ours. We will also explore what the Old Testament and New Testament say about inheritance and why both must be studied to reach a complete picture.

Do read the scriptures mentioned within the devotionals to gain a deeper understanding of these marvellous truths. I believe we have stepped into an era where the choice between self and sacrifice grows wider. Contemplating these truths and letting them take root in our hearts both benefits our lives and impacts the lives of those around us. The bottom line is that we are inheritors of a kingdom filled with plenty. This is both a responsibility and a privilege. I pray heaven's directives are made known to you as you read, just as unexpected concepts were formed while I typed.

What is an heir?

And if children, then heirs – heirs of God and fellow heirs with Christ, provided we suffer with him in order that we may also be glorified with him. (v. 17, ESV)

Let's begin by imagining you suddenly receive a letter in the post requesting your presence at the reading of a will. You drive to the meeting unsure of what to expect and soon find yourself sitting in an ornate office, anxious, curious, and blissfully unaware of the significance or breadth of what you are about to inherit. As the envelope is opened you fidget nervously, and the lawyer begins to read.

We will revisit this scene at the end of our series but suffice to say the forthcoming inheritance affects not only you but also has the potential to affect all your future relationships. We can read more about this inheritance in Romans 8, which is filled with deep and extraordinary truths. Hidden amid this powerful chapter sits our focus for the next few weeks: we are co-heirs with Jesus Christ.

Jesus is the Father's firstborn son (Hebrews 1:6; Psalm 89:27), therefore according to Hebrew law he had rights and privileges as part of the family, rights and privileges we also receive because we are part of the same family. Yes, I know it includes suffering, which we will touch on later, but for now sit with the truth that you have a glorious inheritance not only in heaven but also on earth.

Repeat the following: I am a co-heir with Jesus Christ. Speak it slowly, out loud if possible, planting the seed of truth deep into your spirit. At this moment we are – with all our failings, fears, and uncertainties – an heir to a kingdom that makes all other kingdoms seem like child's play. A kingdom of (truly) undeserved royalty, yet royalty all the same. So, as we begin, adjust your crown, straighten those royal robes, and prepare to plumb the depths of this incredible truth!

If you struggle to see yourself as royalty, ask the Holy Spirit to reveal your true identity during these next few weeks. Write down these truths every day, then look in a mirror and speak what God says, believing his truth over lies.

JEN BAKER

God's original design

So God created man in his own image, in the image of God he created him; male and female he created them. (v. 27, ESV)

I could easily have titled today's devotional 'Where it went wrong', because God's original design went terribly wrong when Adam and Eve changed the course of history through their wilful sin.

Therefore, before we explore the fullness of our inheritance it's important to remember God's original plan for humanity and how that bookends, so to speak, the inheritance we receive. In other words, imagine God's original plan on one side, depravity of sin in the middle, and inheritance on the other side.

In Genesis 1:27 we see that God created humans in his image and his likeness; this means an exact representation. If I'm honest, I find that hard to comprehend. However, in Genesis 1:28–30 scripture goes even further by saying we were created for blessing, fruitfulness, increase, authority, and plenty. Then, in Genesis 2:15, responsibility is added when Adam is put to work in the garden to take care of it. Finally, in Genesis 2:25, the Bible speaks of God's children having no shame but a lifestyle of rest, peace, and unity among one another.

In Genesis 3, everything changes when Adam and Eve overstep their authority and take what was not theirs to take, opening the door to sin and separation from the Father. As a result, the woman received pain and the man toil (3:16–19), putting the ease of their inheritance and authority behind them.

However, though sin entered the world, God's original design never changed. Children living in his likeness has always been his desire. Over the next few weeks, we will discover that the royal benefits and blessings of living as his child remain fully available to all who call on the name of Jesus.

Father, thank you for loving me enough to send your only Son to die for the sins I have committed against you. I repent now of any known sin and choose to receive forgiveness through the blood of Jesus. Amen.

JEN BAKER

Old Testament inheritance

And I will establish my covenant between me and thee and thy seed after thee in their generations for an everlasting covenant, to be a God unto thee, and to thy seed after thee. (v. 7, KJV)

Love always requires sacrifice. Read that sentence again. It is impossible to truly love someone without making sacrifices for them, whether a spouse, friend, child, or the Lord. Living as a believer will require a life of sacrifice. This was beautifully and painfully portrayed in the life of Abraham when God asked him to walk up a mountain and take the life of his miracle boy. Abraham had waited years for this child and yet one word from God was about to destroy all he had believed for. Still, Abraham said yes.

It's important for us to know how inheritance works and especially how it applied in the Old Testament to Abraham and his descendants. The book of Deuteronomy teaches that the firstborn son typically received a double portion of the father's inheritance as a symbol of continuing his father's strength (Deuteronomy 21:17). Equally, it explains that women were not able to receive an inheritance unless there were no sons and they married within the tribe of the father (Numbers 27:8; 36:6).

Today, many laws have changed around inheritance, but this truth remains – inheritance requires death. Woven throughout scripture we see radical obedience walking hand in hand with painful sacrifice. Sacrifice has often been misunderstood, causing many believers to vacillate between boastful prosperity and false humility. Remembering that our inheritance cost us nothing but cost Jesus Christ his life keeps us grounded in true humility and unbridled worship.

Jesus was the seed that died in order to release the inheritance which lets us truly live (Galatians 3:29). May we never tire of that truth. We will explore that idea more tomorrow, but for today, let's position our hearts in a posture of thankfulness for the deep sacrificial love of Jesus Christ.

Jesus, I can never thank you enough for the death you endured to bring me into freedom and relationship with Father, Son, and Spirit. Receive my worship in this moment. Thank you, Jesus. Amen.

JEN BAKER

New Testament inheritance

I will surely bless you, and I will surely multiply your offspring as the stars of heaven and as the sand that is on the seashore. And your offspring shall possess the gate of his enemies, and in your offspring shall all the nations of the earth be blessed. (vv. 17–18, ESV)

Today, let's turn our attention to the New Testament and read several scriptures about inheritance. First, we are no longer slaves (Galatians 4:7) but are free from sin and death. Slavery involves lack of freedom, painful toil, rules, performance, weariness, and little hope for change. The Bible tells us the Father is pleased to give us the kingdom (Luke 12:32), which means the opposite of slavery. As inheritors of his kingdom, we are empowered to live freely and with purpose, to walk in authority, rest from work, and joyfully obey our Father's leading.

You might question how we can expect the promise in Genesis 22 to apply to us when it was given to Abraham. Galatians 3:29 says: 'And if you are Christ's, then you are Abraham's offspring, heirs according to promise'; and Romans 11:17 (NLT) says that anyone who is a child of God has been grafted into the blessing of Abraham. In biblical terms, 'graft' refers to the agricultural practice of joining two plants together so that they grow as one. This remarkable image shows us as born-again believers grafted as one to Abraham, and therefore enjoying the same inheritance.

Our verse for today includes the word 'surely' (v. 17). In other words, blessing is not a possibility but a promise. God is declaring that you can count on and even expect blessings to come. One definition of blessing is 'empowered to prosper' which is exactly what freedom in Christ brings. This does not particularly refer to money, but rather prospering in health, relationships, emotionally, mentally, and spiritually, so we can bring glory to God, overcome the enemy, and help Jesus Christ build his church.

Lord, I choose to place my concerns and fears in your capable hands. Thank you for caring enough to hold them, and hold me, as I sit under the umbrella of your goodness and grace. Amen.

JEN BAKER

Unbelief

So again I ask, does God give you his Spirit and work miracles among you by the works of the law, or by your believing what you heard? So also Abraham 'believed God, and it was credited to him as righteousness.' (vv. 5–6, NIV)

Inheritance in the kingdom is not only about receiving but also about responsibility. The story of the prodigal son (Luke 15:11–32) may be familiar, where one son's wild living squandered the inheritance he was given. Not only that, he also asked for his inheritance before his father had even passed away! You have likely heard stories of families torn apart through inheritance, greed, and the love of money. We read in scripture that the love of money carries with it great evil (1 Timothy 6:10). But this fear of loving money too much has also caused people to embrace a mentality that exalts poverty and shames abundance, which is equally dangerous.

Over many years of studying scripture and breaking wrong mindsets, I have grown to understand that God is a God of abundance. He isn't concerned with how much we have but is very interested in two things: character and generosity. A slaveholder mentality views wealth and resources as a means to maintain control and assert authority, but a slave mentality is also a problem. It's like walking away from the courthouse after receiving a millionaire's inheritance, burying it underground, then submitting again to a cruel master's tyranny of lies, fears, and limitations.

Do you see yourself as a slave or an inheritor? Is your bank balance limited to the world's system or can you see it attached to the storehouses of heaven, which always hold more than enough (2 Corinthians 9:8)? What about your health? Relationships?

Any form of slavery limits another's ability to expand, explore, and dream. Unbelief does the same. The harsh truth is that without crucifying unbelief, our inheritance will never be fully outworked. Abraham's belief in God resulted in generations of blessings. Who and what is on the other side of your belief?

Ask the Holy Spirit to show you any area of your life where unbelief is guiding your decisions or limiting your purpose. Spend time talking to the Lord about this, imagining what life could look like if you truly believed.

JEN BAKER

To receive or not to receive

For the promise to Abraham and his offspring that he would be heir of the world did not come through the law but through the righteousness of faith. (v. 13, ESV)

When a marriage proposal is given, one stands before a nervous, kneeling other half offering a significant life change. The one being asked must fully receive what is being offered for that change to begin. On a smaller scale, we can be offered a perfectly baked scone with as much cream and jam (or jam and cream!) as desired, but unless it's received and enjoyed that scone will decay into something inedible and unwanted. Abraham was positioned though faith and righteousness to receive his inheritance from God, but that wasn't everything. Position was the first step; receiving was the next.

Receiving brings into reality what began as a possibility. Our inheritance has been offered without limit, but it remains unused and ineffective if we don't intentionally receive all that is ours by faith. Abraham was incredulous at the thought of fathering nations at 99 years old with a wife beyond childbearing years. Yet he chose to dig deep into faith and believe a God he knew was faithful.

In our scripture reading Paul makes it clear that the promise made to Abraham was given because of his faith. Similarly, we can never be good enough to earn the inheritance we are promised; we receive it through faith in the precious blood of Jesus Christ and the grace of our loving God (v. 16).

Are you ready to fully receive your inheritance? Abraham received the inheritance not only for himself but also for generations beyond his years. Let me reiterate that our freedom, joy, peace, healing, wholeness, and gifts are meant to overflow to our neighbours, friends, family, and those we will never meet this side of heaven.

Lord, I offer you my life without putting any caveats or restrictions on what you are asking of me. I believe that you are good and that you love me, so I say yes to you today. Amen.

JEN BAKER

Suffering

For I consider that the sufferings of this present time are not worth comparing with the glory that is to be revealed to us. (v. 18, ESV)

Suffering is not a popular topic, yet we cannot separate suffering and the gospel. In fact, the gospel ultimately comes out of the intense and unimaginable suffering endured by our Lord and Saviour.

I recently watched the funeral of President Jimmy Carter. In America he was known for his humanitarian work as much as for his presidency. As a millionaire he could have lived lavishly, but he and his wife of 77 years chose to stay in the first house they ever owned – a bungalow bought in 1961 – until their deaths. President Carter set aside his own comfort to embrace the suffering of others, making a difference with the gifts, resources, and opportunities he was given.

When suffering comes, it's easy to question why, focus inward, and believe our fulfilled life is found on the opposite shores to our current pain. However, the reality is that even in painful seasons we have daily opportunities to use our godly inheritance for the good of others and for the benefit of society. Perhaps when Paul talked of suffering, he was focusing on the opportunity to join in Christ's suffering, rather than focusing on our own challenges.

Read Galatians 2:20. What does it mean to you in light of today's reading? How can suffering and inheritance partner together instead of fighting for dominance in our hearts and minds? I love this thought (paraphrased) from Baptist preacher Alexander MacLaren (1826–1910): when walking the path of suffering, look to see broken twigs in front of you where the Lord has walked before you.

You are not alone on your journey of suffering. Put your suffering heart in his nail-scarred hands and know that the Lord walks this road with you, now until the glorious day you see him face-to-face.

Lord, help me understand your suffering at a deeper level. I want to weep with you over injustice and sit in silence with those who have no words. Today, help me be your hands and feet to the hurting. Amen.

JEN BAKER

Why inheritance matters

Blessed be the God and Father of our Lord Jesus Christ! According to his great mercy, he has caused us to be born again to a living hope through the resurrection of Jesus Christ from the dead, to an inheritance that is imperishable, undefiled, and unfading, kept in heaven for you. (vv. 3–4, ESV)

It's true that our inheritance releases blessings here and now, yet we must not forget the greatest blessing of all – our living hope of eternal life (v. 3). This inheritance cannot become void, shared, or lost but is the joy that awaits every believer the moment they take their last breath. To disregard our eternal inheritance for present blessings is to cheapen the blood of Jesus and grace of God over our lives.

One reason we are tempted to focus on being blessed is our fear of not having enough. Will our needs, healing, relationships, and so on be provided for? I often think of the Israelites who, after 400 years of slavery, left their enslavement with an abundance of riches as they carried the plunder of their enemy out of Egypt (Exodus 12:35–36). God always provides for his children; he is Jehovah Jireh after all! Trusting that God will provide for our current needs, and understanding our future inheritance, frees us to focus on others.

In Titus 3:8 the apostle Paul talks about devoting ourselves to doing good. The word 'devote' could be translated 'practise'; in other words, continually improve in order to mature. When I'm not concerned about my current affairs or provision for the future, I am free to mature in the area of loving my neighbour and doing good by serving others.

John Wesley has been quoted as saying: 'Do all the good you can, by all the means you can, in all the ways you can, in all the places you can, at all the times you can, to all the people you can, as long as ever you can.' Living with eternity in mind allows us to follow Wesley's plea with greater freedom – a freedom that knows, and believes, we are blessed to be a blessing.

What does your eternal inheritance mean to you? Take some time imagining and writing down what you are expecting and why you are eager (if you are) to receive your full inheritance in heaven.

JEN BAKER

Every spiritual blessing

Blessed be the God and Father of our Lord Jesus Christ, who has blessed us in Christ with every spiritual blessing in the heavenly places. (v. 3, ESV)

I encourage you to intentionally meditate on today's passage, because it is rich with truth and empowerment for our day-to-day living. The moment we receive Jesus Christ as our Lord and Saviour we are filled with the Spirit of God who gives us counsel, wisdom, direction, and insight. Spiritual gifts that previously laid dormant come alive and the entirety of God's kingdom becomes legally ours at that moment of adoption into his family – what a thought!

We are reminded in Ephesians 1 that every spiritual blessing in Christ is ours. This includes being chosen, holy, blameless, adopted, redeemed, forgiven, knowing God's will, and being purposed, sealed, and guaranteed an inheritance. Wow, what a list! Insert your name into that list and read it out loud. For example: 'I, Jen, am chosen, holy, blameless…' Read this list repeatedly until you begin seeing yourself as the scriptures describe you. This is how you are seen in heaven!

These truths are not dependent on our good works, achievements, or church attendance. Spiritual blessings belong to us because we belong to Christ. Full stop. Which one do you currently need most? Wisdom? Forgiveness?

In the culture at the time a child biologically related could be disowned from the family, but an adopted child could not, because they were adopted into that family for life. Though we sin, are far from perfect, and need forgiveness every day for our hardness of heart and judgemental attitude, as the Father's adopted daughters we will never be released from our rightful inheritance in the eyes of heaven. Because of this, we can choose each day to receive *all* the spiritual blessings that are ours without limitation. *Selah.*

Lord, my thanks could never be enough for the grace you have given me that is undeserved and often forgotten. Today, help me see myself as you do: wanted, cherished, accepted, and blessed. Amen.

JEN BAKER

Daughter

And he said to her, 'Daughter, your faith has made you well; go in peace, and be healed of your disease.' (v. 34, ESV)

Is there anything in your life that seems to be plaguing you? Any issue physically, emotionally, financially, relationally, or spiritually that has hung on far beyond its expiry date?

At times, our own sin, or the sin of another, enables the enemy to gain a foothold in our lives. Sometimes we make unwise choices which bring unwanted consequences. However, some painful experiences have no answers or explanations, which means the pain goes deeper because we are plagued with not knowing the 'why' as well as with the wound.

We read today about a woman who had been bleeding for twelve years. She had exhausted all means of help from the doctors and was living as an outcast because of her condition. As if pain and continual bleeding weren't enough, she was also isolated and alone.

I love this woman's story because her determination refused to give in to self-pity. When Mark tells us she said, 'I will be healed', the word 'said' (v. 28) in the Greek means to repetitively say. Imagine her approaching Jesus repeating under her breath, 'I will be healed, I will be healed', not allowing doubt or fear a voice as she pressed through the mob that surrounded him.

Upon reaching Jesus, she touched his garments, but this was no ordinary touch. The Greek word for touch means to seize; she literally grabbed hold, extracting the healing power coming from Jesus. This faith is what moved Jesus to speak a word not recorded as being spoken over any other woman in the Bible: 'Daughter.'

Jesus let her (and everyone around her) know that her isolation was finished, her inheritance was secure, and her wholeness had arrived. He speaks the same word over you: 'Daughter'.

Imagine you are pushing through the noise of unbelief and the mob of resistance to bring your impossibility to the power of Jesus. What would you bring? Remember, he only needs a mustard seed of faith to do miracles.

JEN BAKER

Royalty

But you are a chosen race, a royal priesthood, a holy nation, a people for his own possession, that you may proclaim the excellencies of him who called you out of darkness into his marvellous light. (v. 9, ESV)

Growing up in America, I was fascinated by the British royal family. I remember as a twelve-year-old waking up while it was still dark and quietly creeping down the stairs to watch mesmerised as Lady Diana Spencer became a princess when she married Prince Charles. It seemed magical, otherworldly, and like a dream come true.

I love Isaiah 62, where God gives Jerusalem (Zion) a new name and we read, 'You shall be a crown of beauty in the hand of the Lord, and a royal diadem in the hand of your God' (v. 3). What a stunning picture! No coronation crown can compare to the crown of beauty God sees when he looks at us. Whether we feel it or not, the truth of the matter is this: we *are* royal.

The enemy would like us to believe we are slaves, subject to toil, obedience, silence, and a life under the curse of sickness, poverty, and death. Among many passages, Galatians 4 shows us the opposite is true and we are no longer slaves, but daughters of the king (v. 7). Our royalty allows us to choose a relationship out of love not obligation. It's important to remember that we are not tolerated by the Trinity, but desired.

Close your eyes and picture the king's table full of everything that you need (Psalm 23) with the Father, Son and Spirit chatting and laughing as they enjoy the abundance. See yourself sitting at the table with them. Imagine them turning and looking at you, eyes pooled with love, inviting you to take whatever you need and want from their table. It is yours. You belong. You are the daughter of the king. A dream come true.

Lord, thank you for inviting me to your table. Where I feel uncomfortable, be my comfort. When I want to run away, hold my hand. Help me learn what it means to be a royal daughter of the king. Amen.

JEN BAKER

Blessings

And all these blessings shall come upon you and overtake you, if you obey the voice of the Lord your God. (v. 2, ESV)

For many years I desired blessings while simultaneously feeling guilty when I was blessed because I believed that I needed to suffer for the Lord. Therefore, any joy or happiness was nice but not necessary and potentially not beneficial. I believed you had to be serious around the things of God and to desire blessings was at least selfish if not unadulterated greed. It has taken me several years and a deeper study of scripture to understand those thoughts are not from God.

I'm not endorsing unfettered greed or flippant Christianity, but desire is not wrong when positioned under dependence (Psalm 37:4). We often look to our spouse, our children, our friends, our pastor, our finances, the government, the NHS, our jobs or other avenues to be the source of our provision, healing, and protection. True freedom comes when we can, without reservation, know deep in our spirit that only God himself is the true source of all that we need.

What if right now our current need was being held by heaven's hand? What if we're looking around when we need to look up? What if all our fears and anxieties over the future could be swallowed up in one moment of heavenly peace?

I love our verse for today, which says blessings will overtake us. What an amazing picture! Imagine a tsunami of blessings sweeping over us and spilling over to others. How can orphanages be funded, people fed, churches opened, and the poor taken care of if we don't provide them with the resources? Ask for blessings but do so with a focus on the needs of others. We are blessed to be a blessing (Genesis 12:2), but if we shy away from blessings how can we bless?

Imagine the windows of heaven open, pouring out such a blessing that you don't have room to hold all that is falling into your lap (Malachi 3:10). Who would you share this abundance with? Start with what you have now.

JEN BAKER

Eternal purpose

Whatever you do, work heartily, as for the Lord and not for men, knowing that from the Lord you will receive the inheritance as your reward. You are serving the Lord Christ. (vv. 23–24, ESV)

We often think of inheritance as a way to get ahead: to buy our first house; to pay off a debt; to go on holiday; to invest in our future. There is nothing wrong with any of those things, but what portion of our inheritance are we giving back to the kingdom of God? We need to ask this question not only about our financial inheritance but also our spiritual inheritance as a royal priesthood.

A few months ago, while in America, I came face-to-face with death's door. Unbeknown to me I had multiple blood clots throughout both lungs which resulted in pulmonary embolism and emergency surgery. For several days prior to this I was certain anaemia was my problem, so I ate copious amounts of chicken and downed litres of prune juice waiting for the symptoms to ease. (Note to self: never self-diagnose again!)

One evening, at about midnight, I found myself literally fighting for my life. I was alone in the house and at that moment I thought of all I still wanted to do for the kingdom. Suddenly I didn't want a bigger house; I wanted to share the gospel with more people, to see the hurting whole, the sick healed, and the broken restored. Finality brings clarity.

Our inheritance is not only for eternal life, but also for eternal purpose. We have a limited number of days this side of heaven to glorify God by giving him our lives. When was the last time you shared the gospel message with an unbeliever? Who was the last person you discipled? To abdicate our responsibility to the pastor is to reject a direct commandment from the Lord (Matthew 28:18–20). Inheritance is wonderful now and it will be greater in eternity, but we must remember our inheritance is for sharing, not owning.

Father, help me take ownership of the gifts you have given me in order to build disciples and share the good news with my family, friends, and neighbours. Empower me with wisdom and grace as I take steps of faith. Amen.

JEN BAKER

It's guaranteed!

In him you also, when you heard the word of truth, the gospel of your salvation, and believed in him, were sealed with the promised Holy Spirit, who is the guarantee of our inheritance until we acquire possession of it, to the praise of his glory. (vv. 13–14, ESV)

The phrase 'down payment' is another way we could translate the word 'guarantee'. The Holy Spirit is the down payment of a future inheritance. Down payments are put on possessions we want, such as cars or houses, and those down payments guarantee the item will be ours at a future date. What a powerful thought that the Holy Spirit at this moment resides within us as down payment towards an eternal inheritance beyond anything we could dream or imagine!

Sometimes heaven seems too close (see yesterday's devotional), while other times it appears far more distant than we would like. I believe the veil between heaven and earth is paper thin. We need only to stop, quiet the noise, and turn our hearts towards heaven to sense the Spirit of God and presence of the Lord.

I often tell people struggling to discern God's presence to speak the name Jesus out loud, slowly, repeatedly, from their spirit and not their head. Imagine him sitting right next to you, reach out and take his hand, look at the scars, and allow his love to pour oil into your dry and hurting areas. Jesus – the name above all names. Jesus – the one who died leaving us the gift of eternal life. Jesus – our Saviour, our Lord, and our brother.

Let's revisit the office where we began this set of notes, where the lawyer has now opened the will and disclosed its contents. You have received everything, the full inheritance, no questions asked. You sit stunned as you take in all he has said. Suddenly, the lawyer looks pointedly at you and quietly asks, 'What will you do with this inheritance?'

What is your answer?

Lord, thank you for dying so that I can live. Let it go beyond a trite phrase to a deeper truth. As the heir to an unshakeable kingdom, may I not take life for granted but live to serve you alone. Amen.

JEN BAKER

Coping with failure and disappointment

Bridget Plass writes:

Failure and disappointment – not the jolliest subject, is it? But, let's face it, unless we have managed to live a perfect existence, then both are woven into the very fabric of our lives. We use the words all the time to punctuate the simple ups and downs of daily life. 'I was very disappointed the shop had run out of…'! 'Can't believe I failed to remember…'

I failed my driving test three times. Three times did my very disappointed eleven-year-old put the glitter-plastered congratulations card he had made back in the drawer. More seriously, futures can be defined by failing exams or failing to get into university. Marriages fail. Governments fail.

God's profound disappointment with his failing children is a bit of a running theme throughout the Old Testament. Crops failing were signs of his displeasure. Women being infertile was seen as God's punishment. Today we place such blame on random circumstances or on human-induced climate change, but failure still inevitably leads to some degree of disappointment with ourselves and with others. What parent has never said to their children: 'I am extremely disappointed with you!' Who has never felt ashamed of their failure to do what they should have done?

Here is a question: are we allowed to admit sometimes that we are disappointed with God, that deep down we feel he has failed us?

Over the next two weeks we will try to explore truthfully what all this means to us, living as we do in such a chaotic world. We will also look at the ingenious and varied ways God can transfigure our sense of shame and disappointment, recycling it into something useful, if we will come to him just as we are and let the potter do what he does best.

Let's pause a moment and consider if there are things we might need to bring to God over the next few days.

Set to fail

When Moses went and told the people all the Lord's words and laws, they responded with one voice, 'Everything the Lord has said we will do.' Moses then wrote down everything the Lord had said. (vv. 3–4, NIV)

The story of God's people from the beginning until now is littered with well-intentioned promises made and then broken. When God's power was clearly evident, many people became 'mighty men of valour', but usually, except for characters like Joseph and Daniel, it was only for a brief moment in time. Even King David slides down a path so dangerous that it involved murder and potential separation forever from God.

Most of us face less steep inclines, where keeping a foothold seems possible. Nevertheless, unless we block out our increasingly secular world by staying close to people who believe the same as we do, the temptation to abandon open allegiance to Jesus is a constant pressure.

Consider how his very name is used as an expletive in general conversation and the idea of following Jesus is seen as naive and laughable. How easy it is to simply keep quiet about where we stand on certain issues, so we won't rock the boat. How tempting to fudge the truth about how we plan to spend Good Friday and Easter and then back up our story with a little white lie after the weekend. We don't want them to think we're odd, do we? And does it really matter if I join in occasional bits of gossip or laugh about someone behind their back?

Deeply disappointed with ourselves, we can feel sad and ashamed, desperate to reset our relationship with Jesus.

Dear Jesus, we know you too battled with the world's pressures. Thank you for showing us how to take time out with our Father and for teaching us to pray, 'Forgive our trespasses,' and, 'Lead us not into temptation.' Amen.

BRIDGET PLASS

When partial failure is inevitable

'When my master enters the temple of Rimmon to bow down and he is leaning on my arm and I have to bow there also – when I bow down in the temple of Rimmon, may the Lord forgive your servant for this.' 'Go in peace,' Elisha said. (vv. 18–19, NIV)

'Go in peace. Don't worry about it. I understand and so will God.' What must this have meant to Namaan, the powerful man whose life had been overshadowed by leprosy.

He had arrived at Elisha's door laden with goods, fully expecting to do business with the prophet and with his powerful God. However, the treatment he was prescribed was not what he had expected, and he had stomped off in a rage. Fortunately, he listened to his servants, bathed in the inferior river and was completely healed. He could now return to his wife and his job as leader of the army a new man. Except it wasn't that simple. It wasn't just Naaman's skin that had been changed. Now Namaan had a new master – the God of Elisha was now his God, and he was determined to worship only him. There's just one small problem!

We always have at least one small problem, don't we – or perhaps several. When is it right to compromise? When should we take a stand? The early church had similar problems and sought advice about sharing meals with people who still sacrificed their meat to false gods. Paul counselled that they should be flexible, but try, with the help of the Holy Spirit, to stay clean inside (1 Corinthians 8).

The prophet Micah taught God's people 'to act justly and to love mercy and to walk humbly with your God' (Micah 6:8). Perhaps for us, avoiding gossip, back biting, and thinking we know best may be a good way to start.

Dear Father, thank you for Elisha's words. Help us to believe that, if we are trying our best, maybe we too can happily 'go in peace, to love and serve the Lord'. Amen.

BRIDGET PLASS

Visible and invisible

Now Eli the priest was sitting on his chair by the doorpost of the Lord's house. In her deep anguish Hannah prayed to the Lord, weeping bitterly… As she kept on praying to the Lord, Eli observed her mouth. Hannah was praying in her heart, and her lips were moving but her voice was not heard. Eli thought she was drunk. (vv. 9–10, 12–13, NIV)

Let's face it, all visible addictions are easy prey to those who have never understood the grip and comfort of things such as smoking, or to those who need to criticise others to avoid facing their own secret failures, or to those who avoid involvement by simply offering spiritual platitudes. In Hannah's case, her despair is based on never having anything visible! She has failed to get pregnant, which was considered a punishment from God and opened her up to yearly taunting by her husband's second (child-bearing) wife, Penninah.

Hannah's disappointment leads her to run to the temple and pour out her feelings to the only one who can help her. If ever we need proof that God always has a plan, this is it. The hopes of not one but two broken people are about to be renewed. Listening at the door is someone equally crippled by disappointment: Eli, failed father of Hophni and Phinehas, who are a disgrace to the priesthood. Needing to vent his pent-up anger on someone else, he chastises this apparently drunk stranger for behaving inappropriately in his place of worship. Her sad, dignified response breaks through to his spirit and his heart goes out to her. Now both have been given a second chance: Hannah to bear a child, Samuel; Eli to play a part in the upbringing of a future prophet.

There are a thousand new beginnings with God. Maybe we can be kinder to non-overcomers, including ourselves, allowing our failures to go to God and our hearts to go out to whoever needs our understanding.

BRIDGET PLASS

Best laid plans of mice and men

'Don't call me Naomi,' she told them. 'Call me Mara, because the Almighty has made my life very bitter. I went away full, but the Lord has brought me back empty.' (vv. 20–21, NIV)

Sometimes life can make you want to scream at God: 'It just isn't fair!' No one knew this more than Naomi, whose name literally means 'pleasant'. She and her husband Elimelek, with their two sons Mahlon and Kilion, had made what they considered a perfectly reasonable decision to leave the famine in Judah and seek a better life in Moab. Both sons had married Moabite women, and the future looked bright. Then tragedy struck not once but three times. First Elimelek, then Mahlon and finally Kilion died. Naomi was left with two daughters-in-law and no male protectors.

Apparently forsaken by God, her only option was to return, a failure, to Bethlehem. She managed to persuade Orpah to reluctantly go back to her mother, but Ruth stubbornly insisted on going with her, even vowing that Naomi's God would become hers.

It can't have been a very happy journey! Bitterness is growing in Naomi like a poisonous weed, and when they arrive in her hometown all her pent-up hurt explodes. If you are familiar with this story, you will know that Naomi hasn't been totally forgotten by God. She will know security and joy again as Ruth and her future husband Boaz will give her a grandchild, Obed, to help fill the hole left by her beloved sons. But right now, she needs to vent her feelings.

How often do we try to put a positive spin on our life's downturns because we are either afraid of upsetting God or don't want to give him a bad reference to unbelievers?

If you are hurting, could you take a leaf out of Naomi's book and trust God with what's really going on inside and tell it straight? The Bible assures us that God loves us enough to deal with it!

BRIDGET PLASS

When we get on the wrong train

'But do not do what they do, for they do not practise what they preach. They tie up heavy, cumbersome loads and put them on other people's shoulders, but they themselves are not willing to lift a finger to move them. Everything they do is done for people to see.' (vv. 3–5, NIV)

This is Jesus on the attack. He is challenging shepherds who have failed to safeguard their sheep and their petty man-made rules that distort the truth that ordinary people have always mattered to God. He criticises teaching that leads people into danger, honours empty sacrifice over care and love, and has created a structure based on power, wealth, and outward appearance.

It happened then and it happens now. The trappings of Christianity can become elevated above the needs of the people. Leaders become celebrities. Worship leaders are worshipped. Heavy shepherding is accepted, weighing people down and sapping individual creativity and joy. Rules exclude the vulnerable from being welcomed into the church family or demand that you set aside any doubts and abandon critical thinking, insisting that you accept the authority of whatever you are being taught.

The Lutheran theologian Dietrich Bonhoeffer once said: 'If you board the wrong train, it is no use running along the corridor in the other direction.' Sometimes the only answer is to get off the train.

When you do, you may find yourself on the platform of a disused little tumbleweed country station with no idea where you are and all familiar bearings gone. You may feel you have become an outcast and lost your friends. The getting back to where you first began may mean you get scarred by brambles, muddied, exhausted, and hungry. But Jesus came to seek out and find those who are lost (Luke 19:10), so you will be found. You will get safely to a place where you are able to start out again, this time a little wiser.

Dear Lord, help us to recognise when things are not as they should be and give us the courage to find our way back to you. Amen.

BRIDGET PLASS

If I was God

'Which of you fathers, if your son asks for a fish, will give him a snake instead? Or if he asks for an egg, will give him a scorpion? If you then, though you are evil, know how to give good gifts to your children, how much more will your Father in heaven give the Holy Spirit to those who ask him!' (vv. 11–13, NIV)

I know I'm not the only one to have found this passage bewildering. Obviously, we are not going to be doling out dangerous snakes and scorpions to those in our care when they clearly need the equivalent of nourishing fish and eggs! We want the very best for them – their health and happiness and freedom from whatever pain and worry they are experiencing. Sometimes all we can offer is our love and time and maybe gifts to cheer them up. But this is God we are talking about, and he has the power, as demonstrated by Jesus many times, to radically change situations. Surely if we hammer on his door often enough, he will give us what we are asking. After all, he is our Father. He loves us and those we love, doesn't he?

Sometimes the miracle we have begged him for occurs, but I meet too many people suffering devastating disappointments – not only a heart-breaking situation not resolved but also a Father who didn't appear to care. On occasion, this leads to a complete breakdown in the relationship, and they declare they will never speak to God or trust him again.

Let's look again at what Jesus actually said. 'How much more will your Father in heaven give the Holy Spirit to those who ask him!' (v. 13). Jesus isn't talking about health and wealth, although that may be included. He is talking about the Holy Spirit, the extraordinary gift that keeps on giving. God's Spirit brings the possibility of peace into the most difficult times in our lives and offers to walk with us into every place we find ourselves. He will shoulder the weight of our pain and help us to laugh and to cry. Is that worth hammering at the door again for?

Dear Holy Spirit, thank you for the many times you have been there for me, even speaking for me to my Father, especially when I have no hope and no words left. Amen.

BRIDGET PLASS

Deaf to the call

The one who enters by the gate is the shepherd of the sheep... He calls his own sheep by name and leads them out. When he has brought out all his own, he goes on ahead of them, and his sheep follow him because they know his voice. (vv. 2–4, NIV)

Do we, though? Always know? Perhaps one of our greatest fears is the likelihood of our failure to recognise the voice of the good shepherd, living as we do in a world full of noise.

When my elderly mother needed replacement hearing aids, I drove her to the nearest centre, which was in a large shopping mall. Coming out after her test, her face was contorted with panic as she struggled to hear me calling her, confused by the cacophony of noise battering her ears. Her brain had not yet discerned the difference between ignorable backward noises and the sounds she needed to hear. What if God has been trying to get through, but we've been too busy or distracted to hear? What if we've got it wrong, and we are trotting happily along behind someone who looks and sounds authentic but is in fact a 'hired hand' who will abandon us if they 'see the wolf coming'?

Our problems are compounded by the fact there never was one clear way God has chosen to communicate. From a burning bush to bellowing from a fiery, smoky mountain, a whisper after a mighty wind to a voice in the night to a young boy, and then dreams, visions, angels – no wonder Jesus realised we would need a good hearing aid to help us discern his voice and promised us the free gift of his Spirit.

Of course we will get it wrong, deafened by our raucous world, our desperate desires, or our wilful selective hearing, but Jesus won't give up on us.

Dear Jesus, help us to believe that, like all true shepherds you will never stop looking for us, never stop calling us to help this broken world, and never give up on us till we are safely home. Amen.

BRIDGET PLASS

When we turn away

He went on to say, 'This is why I told you that no one can come to me unless the Father has enabled them.' From this time many of his disciples turned back and no longer followed him. (vv. 65–66, NIV)

I am about to confess something! I understand the many reasons why people turn back and no longer follow Jesus. Those who said then and say now: 'You said you are the bread of life and if I come to you, I won't ever be hungry. But I came to you, I joined you and I still hunger.' Those who jeered then, 'Hang on, I know your mum and dad,' and now might say, 'I know your tribe. They are a mean, judgemental crowd. Can't trust any of you.'

Then there are those, both then and now, who have been confused by teaching diametrically opposed to everything they have been taught. The rich young ruler who had ticked every box he could think of and wondered if there was just one more that would guarantee him eternal life. 'Give up everything and follow you? Throw away everything I have built up which gives me the status of success? I don't think so.'

The disappointed list continues. All those brought up by their parents to be independent and now taught that they must do the opposite and learn to be completely dependent on God. Followers then and now who expected powerful intervention in the world as they knew it, unable to accept the concept of necessary suffering and a powerless Christ on the cross.

So many disappointed people walking sadly away. But there have always been those who follow Jesus 'despite' as well as 'because', who don't fudge the issue of their bewilderment and disappointment but allow themselves to remember the times when the Father enabled them to believe it was the only way.

Can we join Peter in saying, 'To whom shall we go? You have the words of eternal life' (v. 68). If not, pray this simple prayer: Please, Father, help our unbelief. Amen.

BRIDGET PLASS

When we look back

A dispute also arose among them as to which of them was considered to be greatest. (v. 24, NIV)

How must the disciples have felt as they looked back to their last Passover meal with Jesus? Could they really have been arguing about who was the greatest, like children squabbling at the dinner table, only hours away from Jesus' death?

Do you have a memory that pops up and overwhelms you with shame? I have several! One in particular makes me squirm every time I allow myself to think about it. My husband and I once travelled to Bangladesh with World Vision to discover whether child sponsorship really did make a difference. It also gave us a chance to meet our sponsored child, Shanaj, who was eleven years old and lived with her mum in a slum on the outskirts of Dhaka.

Sitting in their tiny shack, I gave out the small gifts I had brought with me from England. I confess I was excited to see their reaction. Then Shanaj's mum opened hers. 'What do I do with these?' she inquired, looking with excited puzzlement at the box of prettily wrapped small squares. That was when the horror of what I had brought sunk in. I had given scented bath cubes to a woman who had no bath or bathroom – no water at all, in fact. She had to wash her clothes, body, and hair in the dirty gutter outside in the street. How I wish I could erase the memory or go back to put it right.

I meet many people who wish they had the chance to do just this, especially before someone unexpectedly dies. Unfortunately, we can't turn back the clock, but perhaps we can learn from our mistakes, so we don't make the same mistake again.

Dear Father, help us to accept that we will never match up to our ideals, and help us not to despair but resolve to be wiser next time and give ourselves just as we are to you. Amen.

BRIDGET PLASS

When we promise too much

'Simon, Simon, Satan has asked to sift all of you as wheat. But I have prayed for you, Simon, that your faith may not fail. And when you have turned back, strengthen your brothers.' But he replied, 'Lord, I am ready to go with you to prison and to death.' (vv. 31–33, NIV)

We know Peter meant what he said with every bone in his body. In the garden of Gethsemane, he was ready with his sword to defend Jesus, and he followed the crowd into the courtyard. Then came the moment when it all went wrong. The realisation of what was happening to his dearest friend, combined with the horror of what might happen to him, proved to be his undoing.

Afterwards, during that famous breakfast on the beach, Jesus reinstates Peter and assures him that he still has work for him to do: 'Feed my sheep' (John 21:17).

So, Peter did just that, no doubt with a sadder but more realistic view of the dangers of relying on wishful thinking. If he hadn't known what it was to reach rock bottom, would he have been able to genuinely feed anyone or strengthen his brothers? Would he have been open to a particular dream that would change the world (Acts 10:9–48)?

I expect we've all had times when we have not been able to live up to our own expectations and promised more than we were able to fulfil. I remember one of the only times I managed to face this and head it off at the pass. A close friend was experiencing the devastating loss of her sister, and I so wanted to be her number one support. I wanted to say to her: 'I will be by your side whenever you need me day or night', but what I actually said was: 'I know I will let you down. I won't be with you at three o'clock in the morning when you need me most.' The hug that followed was sad but real, and I was free to get on with the job of being her friend as best I could.

Dear Father, we so want to be more than we are. Help us to trust that you can still use us to feed your sheep despite us being decidedly less than perfect. Amen.

BRIDGET PLASS

When we pass the buck

When [Pilate] learned that Jesus was under Herod's jurisdiction, he sent him to Herod, who was also in Jerusalem at that time. (v. 7, NIV)

What relief it must have been for embattled Pilate to discover the troubling problem standing in front of him could become someone else's! Herod Antipas was the son of Herod the Great (the man responsible for slaughtering all the baby boys in Bethlehem at the time of Jesus' birth) and ruled over Galilee. Since Jesus was Galilean, Pilate could legitimately send him to Herod and avoid having to deal with him.

Herod, however, found a non-miracle performing Jesus a disappointing gift and, after enjoying ridiculing him, sent him back!

Many years ago, my husband ran a secure unit for extremely damaged and challenging teenagers, some of whom had been let down by a series of decisions. After an urgent and understandable removal from a problem home, there followed a stint in foster care, which often broke down irretrievably and led to a move to a children's home and then to a specialist children's centre. Each time a meeting would agree that the present placement was not appropriate for this particular child's needs and the 'buck' would be passed – a continual rejection fuelling the child's disastrous downward spiral.

I know I have sometimes held internal meetings with myself in which 'we' have agreed the problem facing 'us' is not ours to pursue! Sometimes it was because I knew I lacked the skills or commitment it required, but on other occasions it was simply that I failed to resist the temptation to 'pass the buck'.

How often do we try to dodge playing our part – even when we know deep down it's our name on the job ticket: our place to be our church's welcome even if we're not on the rota, to open our home whether convenient or not, to be loving even we don't feel it?

Dear Father, please don't give up on us! Help us to start again to accept the challenge of being the eyes and ears and heart of Jesus, whatever it takes. Amen.

BRIDGET PLASS

When there's still a job to do

Now Joseph was a disciple of Jesus, but secretly because he feared the Jewish leaders. With Pilate's permission, he came and took the body away. He was accompanied by Nicodemus, the man who earlier had visited Jesus at night... Taking Jesus' body, the two of them wrapped it, with the spices, in strips of linen. (vv. 38–40, NIV)

Sometimes it is all over – the hopes, the dreams, the hard work, the loyalty, the excitement. It may be something or someone we have prayed in earnest for – a community project, a church plant, a personal goal, or a person who didn't get healed. We believed God was in it with us, but it's all apparently ended in failure, leaving us disappointed and often despairing.

In our passage today, we read about the death of Jesus. This amazing storyteller, miracle-maker, hypocrisy attacker, and friend was someone who many had believed was their Saviour who would rescue Israel. The women in his life, with all hope gone, stood at the foot of the cross so he would not die alone. Now we meet two people who have been standing in the wings, not brave enough to step on to the stage until now.

Joseph of Arimathea had plucked up enough courage to ask Pilate for the mangled body of Jesus and offered his own tomb as a safe place for it to lie. Nicodemus had brought spices so that respect could be paid with appropriate dignity. Normally a family would insist on a grand noisy funeral procession led by women with loud wailing, flautists, and professional mourners. Here we find two bit players carefully and gently carrying Jesus secretly to Joseph's garden tomb.

To those of us who have felt ashamed that they didn't give enough support while hope was alive, didn't pray enough or care enough, and thus perhaps even contributed to the failure, take courage. There may still be a vital job waiting to be done.

Dear Lord, we are sorry for the times we have disappointed you by not stepping up in the past. Please can you find a walk-on part for us now? We really want to be extras in your ongoing drama. Amen.

BRIDGET PLASS

When grief blinds you

Now that same day two of them were going to a village called Emmaus, about seven miles from Jerusalem. They were talking with each other about everything that had happened. As they talked and discussed these things with each other, Jesus himself came up and walked along with them; but they were kept from recognising him. (vv. 13–16, NIV)

I know it has been suggested that there could have been a practical reason for the two disciples' inability to recognise their walking companion. Maybe the setting sun was in their eyes, as I know from experience when driving. But really? The two disciples were sad and upset. Jesus was dead! They had been there. They had seen it. And everything they had hoped for had died with him. Common sense combined with their profound disappointment and grief blinded them as comprehensively as Mary's tears in the garden temporarily prevented her from recognising her dearest friend.

The disciples' grief would soon turn to joy, but very often our disappointments are not resolved in such a wonderful way. In some circumstances – the death of a child, the breakdown of a marriage, illness or severe disability, dementia, loneliness, depression – tears may be part of our lives for as long as we live, and we must accept the harshest of realities – that life can never be the same again. Our sadness will not be resolved by a miracle, and we may feel blind to any possibility that spring will come again.

However, I have witnessed the miracle of friendship again and again over the years. Having someone who is prepared to walk closely alongside us through our darkest winters might mean we will one day be able to begin to see new colours through our tears.

Dear Father, help us to tentatively walk forward instead of standing still. Help us to continue to show hospitality and have little holidays from our grief to share memories and even have a good laugh together. Amen.

BRIDGET PLASS

When failure is the key to success

Meanwhile, the witnesses laid their coats at the feet of a young man named Saul. While they were stoning him, Stephen prayed, 'Lord Jesus, receive my spirit.' Then he fell on his knees and cried out, 'Lord, do not hold this sin against them.' (vv. 58–60, NIV)

The blasphemy about Jesus is being repeated by this young upstart. It needs stamping out as quickly as possible and you, Saul, have done it. Well done, you! But as you stood there, coats at your feet, calmly watching the agonising death of this young man, questions must be battering at the closed doors of your faith. Why isn't he begging for mercy? How can he be asking for forgiveness for his executioners? Whom or what is he looking at with his eyes shining?

Everything up to that point had been so clear cut, hadn't it? Highly educated and steeped in the correctness of Judaism, what Saul was witnessing didn't fit the pattern. Certainty can appear strong and invincible, but it is brittle, and when a crack appears the whole structure is likely to shatter.

Determined to stamp on any signs of weakness in his armour, Saul set out to destroy the followers of The Way. If we are familiar with the story of the early church, we know that crack will be torn open wide by Jesus himself on that famous road to Damascus (9:1–19). Saul would later become known as the apostle Paul, who dedicated his life to spreading the gospel of Jesus.

Stephen died as he lived. He was the real deal, full of the Spirit, confident in the truth, and full of hope in his future. What about us? Dare we discard the certainties we have always relied on, face the many times we got things terribly wrong, shake off disappointment with ourselves, and start again?

Dear Jesus, help us to stuff all our doubts, failures, uncertainties, disappointments, questions, and failures into our backpacks and follow, trusting only you for our future safety. Amen.

BRIDGET PLASS

The faithfulness of God

Sheila Jacobs writes…

What do you think of when you think about faithfulness? Perhaps a spouse who doesn't look at another person? Maybe someone who serves in church every Sunday, often without recognition, or a friend who is always there to help pick up the pieces when we get it wrong?

How would you define God's faithfulness? We have probably all known times when fervent prayer hasn't been answered – at least, not in the way we'd hoped. Does that make us question the faithfulness of God?

When my mother was dying, a friend took me to see her to say goodbye because I had an eye condition which meant I couldn't drive. My mum had had dementia for many years, and when I'd last seen her, she hadn't recognised me or known she had a daughter at all. However, as she lay dying and I held her hand, she knew me. We talked about Jesus and, as we did so, I suddenly had the urge to sing that wonderful old hymn 'Great is thy faithfulness'. Now, I'm not a good singer, but on that occasion, I (miraculously!) appeared to be in tune and my mother joined in with the chorus.

We finished singing, and there was a feeling of heaven in that little room. It was a terribly sad situation, but there was peace. It was the last time I saw her. She's with Jesus now.

My mother suffered with many medical conditions towards the end of her life: she couldn't walk or stand to support her own weight and she had Parkinson's disease, heart and kidney problems, and vascular dementia. How then could we sing 'Great is thy faithfulness'? When she first became ill, the promise I'd had from Jesus was that he was 'in it with me'. And amazingly, my mum used to speak of him and the joy of his presence, even on her frailest days.

I can't explain the mysteries of life and the suffering and disappointments we experience on earth, but I know God is faithful, and I have experienced that faithfulness in many different ways.

Over the next couple of weeks, we'll be thinking about Thomas Chisholm's lovely hymn, based on Lamentations 3:23, as we explore the topic of God's faithfulness, especially through the storms of life. I hope as you read these notes, you will be as encouraged as I have been in writing them.

True nature

God is love. This is how God showed his love among us: he sent his one and only Son into the world that we might live through him. (vv. 8–9, NIV)

I'm sure you can remember times in your life when someone who loved you protected and helped you when things were difficult. I can recall a time when I was a child and had meandered off into a wood with a friend and their dad to do some fishing. My parents had told me to be back by a certain time, so when that time approached, I began to walk back along the path that I hoped would lead me out of the unfamiliar wood. Just as I was beginning to get scared, I suddenly saw my dad wandering down the path to meet me. I was so relieved and felt so loved and protected.

1 John 4:8 tells us that 'God is love'. When we realise that this is who he is – his very nature – we can begin to understand something of his faithfulness. 1 Corinthians 13:8 tells us that 'love never fails'. If God is all love, then his thoughts and actions towards us will be love. Love 'always protects' (1 Corinthians 13:7) and wants what is best for us.

It can be hard at times to see that God's delays in answering prayer can be part of his faithfulness to us. Understanding the fundamental nature of God, who loves us so much that he sent his own Son to rescue us from eternal separation from him, at such a huge cost, is to see one who always works for our good – if we allow him. It's worth re-reading John 3:16–17 and allowing those words to soak into our very being, as we recall his goodness to us.

The hymn that we will be exploring in these notes, 'Great is thy faithfulness', speaks of the true nature of God. And it all starts with love.

Think about one area in your life – past or present – where you can see the love of God towards you, demonstrated in a special way. Spend a few moments thanking him for it!

SHEILA JACOBS

Great love

Because of the Lord's great love we are not consumed, for his compassions never fail. They are new every morning; great is your faithfulness. (vv. 22–23, NIV)

The journey of life is not an easy one. I'm sure we can all remember times of affliction, trouble, or when we have wandered away from God into a wilderness and the heaviness of heart that accompanies such times. It could be that even today we are navigating a difficult road. However, if we know Jesus, there's a good reason not to despair. Why? Because his 'great love' for us will mean the difficulties and challenges will not consume us.

The issues of life can appear overwhelming. But when we feel as if we are sinking, like Peter when he walked on the water (Matthew 14:22–32), we need to just lift our eyes and call out for help. Peter felt the strong hand of Jesus pulling him out of the depths, and we can experience that too.

It's wonderful to know that God has compassion on us; he knows that we are frail creatures who often wander off like sheep and need the shepherd to find and rescue us. I for one am very grateful that God's mercies are new 'every morning'. His faithfulness means that I can wait on him to deliver me, and even if that deliverance seems delayed, I know that, because of his great love he will not abandon me.

The verses we have read today encourage 'self-talk': 'I say to myself' (v. 24). It's good to remind ourselves who the Lord is and to wait for him to act on our behalf. Waiting quietly for God to act isn't easy, but believing in his love and compassion, and so then relying on his faithfulness is a powerful step in our walk of faith.

Lord, help me to remember that it is because of your great love that I will not be consumed! Jesus, today I commit to you [name any specific issue]. Thank you, Lord, for hearing me. I wait on you. Amen.

SHEILA JACOBS

O God my Father

To Titus, my true son in our common faith: Grace and peace from God the Father and Christ Jesus our Saviour. (v. 4, NIV)

What a beautiful start to a letter! Paul talks about a God 'who does not lie', who keeps promises and in whom we have the hope of eternity (v. 2). If God has promised something, it will happen. He sent a Saviour, one to take away all that separates us from him, and because of this, we know we can have life beyond the confines of this earth. Jesus is our Saviour; he is the 'resurrection and the life' (John 11:25), and we know that if we trust in him, we can have that eternal relationship with God, beginning right now.

The issue of God being our Father can be troublesome for some people. We tend to run things through our own filter, so if we have had fathers who were absent, unloving, or punishing, we might think that God is the same. However, God is a perfect Father, and Jesus encouraged us to pray to him as Father in the family prayer he taught us in Matthew 6:9–13.

The hymn we are looking at in these notes talks about the faithfulness of 'God my Father'. Earthly fathers can let us down or we may not even have known them, but God will not fail or forsake us (1 Chronicles 28:20).

When we come into relationship with Jesus, we can call God 'Our Father'. Both Romans 8:15 and Galatians 4:6 assert that we have a new relationship with God through Jesus, and that we are part of his family. This means we also have new brothers and sisters to accompany us on our journey. In Paul's letter to Titus, Paul refers to Titus as his 'true son' in the faith. We're part of a bigger network of people who all have the same Father!

Slowly recite the Lord's Prayer as found in Matthew 6. What part of the prayer especially speaks to you today?

SHEILA JACOBS

No shadow of turning

Your love, Lord, reaches to the heavens, your faithfulness to the skies… How priceless is your unfailing love, O God! People take refuge in the shadow of your wings. (vv. 5–7, NIV)

In this psalm, the writer, David, sings of the unbounded graciousness of God! His heart is lifted towards his faithful God, who is far above all his enemies and his troubles. David says that people can 'take refuge' in God (v. 7). He is like a fortress, and we can run to him and be safe, trusting him to take care of us.

But what if we feel we have let him down? Perhaps we think that if we were to turn to him in our crisis or loneliness, after neglecting our relationship with him for months or years – or maybe even ignored the very fact that he offered relationship with us at all – he would reject us.

Thankfully, as we read in this hymn, there is no 'shadow of turning' in our Lord. We can see this so clearly in the story of the prodigal son (Luke 15). The boy disrespects his father, runs away, and finds himself in deep trouble. On returning home, he expects to be received as a servant and not a son, but he experiences the overarching love of his father, who is so delighted to have him back that he throws a party! What a wonderful picture of our loving heavenly Father.

God doesn't turn away from us, and he doesn't ignore our needs. As we commit everything to him, we can expect him to work for our good and his glory. Even if it looks as if he has momentarily stepped away from us, we can be assured that he has not forgotten us. Remember the promise of Jesus: 'All those the Father gives me will come to me, and whoever comes to me I will never drive away' (John 6:37).

Does God seem a long way away? Do you feel you have failed him? Turn to him and receive his love. He's waiting!

SHEILA JACOBS

Thou changest not

Every good and perfect gift is from above, coming down from the Father of the heavenly lights, who does not change like shifting shadows. (v. 17, NIV)

We're concentrating here on the God who doesn't change (see Malachi 3:6), but we are changeable creatures, often acting like weathervanes in a storm. Sometimes we make promises and find that we are unable or unwilling to keep them. Perhaps we have been let down by people who have changed their minds about something they promised us or even how they feel about us.

The picture here of shadows shifting is a powerful one. When we come with our requests to God, we need to take him seriously. He is not capricious like the ancient Roman or Greek gods. He has revealed in his word who he is and what he is like. Ultimately, he has revealed himself in Jesus, who is the 'exact representation' of his very being (Hebrews 1:3).

Our God supplies good and perfect gifts, and when we ask him for wisdom, we should do so believing he will answer us (v. 5). In today's passage, the writer admonishes us – for we need to believe, not doubt, when we make requests of God. However, though he is generous, we need to remember that God knows what is best for us.

Sometimes we don't need to know why we are being asked to do (or not to do) something; we just need to trust the person giving the instructions. It's the same with God; we may not always understand why he answers our prayers (or not) as he does, but we need to trust the one we call on.

Let's have faith when we pray to him, trusting that he is good, that he loves us, and that he knows the plans he already has for us (Jeremiah 29:11). The more we step out in trust, the greater our faith will grow.

Unchanging one, I give you praise. Help me to not be double-minded when I pray, to ask and not doubt that you answer, and to trust you. Amen.

SHEILA JACOBS

Thy compassions, they fail not

As a father has compassion on his children, so the Lord has compassion on those who fear him; for he knows how we are formed, he remembers that we are dust. (vv. 13–14, NIV)

We have been looking at different aspects of God: how he is love, our Father, unchanging, and trustworthy.

In Psalm 103, David is praising a God who forgives our sins (v. 3), heals us (v. 3), redeems us (v. 4), and satisfies us (v. 5). David also praises God because he 'remembers that we are dust' (v. 14). I'm glad God remembers that, because I so often get it wrong.

The faithfulness of God in forgiving our sins is overwhelming. He is holy and perfect, and we are not. In Genesis we read that our ancestors, who walked with God, made a tragic error and blocked their friendship with him, separating themselves (and future generations) from his loving presence. God made provision for his people's forgiveness through animal sacrifices, but in his great compassion, he then sent his only Son so that he would be the fulfilment of the law – the one who, both human and divine, could pay the price humanity owed. Only a human could pay the price for humankind's sin; only a sinless God could live a perfect life and lay it down for us.

It's good to keep short accounts with God. In his first letter, John says that 'if we confess our sins, he is faithful and just and will forgives us our sins and purify us from all unrighteousness' (1 John 1:9). We need to keep in step with the Holy Spirit, maintaining that close walk with God.

God calls us to freedom – freedom to choose to obey him, to live in love, and to know that because of Jesus, we are not condemned. We have a 'faithful high priest' in Jesus, who made 'atonement' for our sins, and because he was a man, as well as God, understands our frailty (Hebrews 2:17–18).

Spend some time before God, bringing before him anything you know you need to say sorry for. Thank him for his faithfulness in forgiving you. Then praise him – perhaps with David's words from Psalm 103!

SHEILA JACOBS

Thou forever wilt be

'I am the Alpha and the Omega, the First and the Last, the Beginning and the End.' (v. 13, NIV)

God has no beginning and no end; he is the Alpha and the Omega. 'As thou hast been, thou forever wilt be', as the hymn tells us. We, as human beings, live within God-given time. We note the passage of the days, the weeks, the years; we grow old, and we ultimately pass away. But that's not the end.

Jesus said, 'Very truly I tell you, whoever obeys my word will never see death' (John 8:51), and he promised 'eternal life' to all those who would believe in him (John 3:16).

We cannot begin to imagine what eternal life will look like once we have stepped from this life into the next. But we can trust the one who tells us that he himself is the way, the truth and the life, and that the way to peace with God is through him alone (John 14:6). We can't earn eternal life through good works – although good works should follow us, once we trust in God and let his Spirit live in and through us.

Only an eternal being could gift us eternity. Ephesians 2:8 tells us that it is by 'grace' – God's free, unearned favour – that we are saved, 'through faith – and this is not from yourselves, it is the gift of God'. It's only by the blood of Christ, shed for us in the ultimate act of atonement, that we can receive the gifted righteousness that covers our sin and shame.

We wait for the day when Jesus returns; when the one who is 'Faithful and True' in his very nature (Revelation 19:11) will make everything new. Come, Lord Jesus!

Lord, thank you that you are the eternal one, who gives eternal life to all who ask you for it. We can never begin to thank you enough. Praise you, Lord! Amen.

SHEILA JACOBS

New mercies I see

Surely your goodness and love will follow me all the days of my life, and I will dwell in the house of the Lord forever. (v. 6, NIV)

Sometimes it's only as we look back, like surveying a valley from a hilltop, that we can see the goodness and love of God that has followed us. It isn't always apparent when we're travelling through darker times, wondering where God is, and if he will ever show up again. That's why it's good to stop and review our lives to date and give thanks to the good shepherd of David's famous psalm.

If we have journeyed with Jesus for a long time, we can start to take God's gracious mercies for granted. When I was growing up, my family didn't go to church, and although I had a good upbringing, a living relationship with Jesus wasn't part of it until I was older. I remember being terrified at a school where I just wasn't coping academically and then suddenly having a 'God encounter' and knowing he was real. Within a matter of months, my family had relocated to a different part of the country, and I had a wonderful fresh start. Now, I see God's hand in that; but I also see times before then when God didn't feature at all in my thinking or experience. I was miserable, scared, and alone. What would my life have been like if the good shepherd hadn't broken into it with his love and mercy?

When we face difficult times, we can have confidence that God is with us, even if we don't feel his presence, because he is faithful. Jesus didn't promise us an easy life (John 16:33), but he did promise he would always be with us (Matthew 28:20). Looking back over our lives, it may lift our spirits to remember his mercies of days past, see his trail of goodness and love, and look forward to his new mercies of today and tomorrow.

Think about your life over the past week. What 'new mercies' can you see?

SHEILA JACOBS

All I have needed

'Therefore do not worry about tomorrow, for tomorrow will worry about itself. Each day has enough trouble of its own.' (v. 34, NIV)

In these notes, we are exploring the faithfulness of God, and provision is certainly one area where I have found God to be faithful. When I was ill, I lived a frugal life, but my needs were met. When I needed employment and couldn't get a job due to life-limiting agoraphobia, God provided work I could do at home. So why, then, do I still fret about things? I think it's because I just don't spend enough time with my heavenly Father, remembering and recalling his goodness, and growing in faith and trust as I draw near to him and he draws near to me (James 4:8). Listening is a huge part of that.

So often when we pray, we present God with a shopping list. Many times, my prayers are a lot of things I'd like God to do for me. I say thank you, tell him what I want, then it's as if I put the phone down without waiting to listen to what God has to say! I don't actually seek his will in a matter. It's more 'My will be done' than 'Yours'. More importantly, I don't seek him purely for his presence.

How would it be if we spoke to a friend in this way? Told them what they could do for us, and then put the phone down without actually interacting with them? I don't think that friendship would last long!

We often forget that our relationship with God is a two-way street. Listening to him, finding out what his will is in a situation or decision, big or small, means we must stay close, learning to discern his voice (John 10:27), and ultimately trusting him to provide all that we need – which might not always be what we think we need!

How much time do you spend listening to God? Think about ways you can facilitate a space in your day to just listen to him – perhaps on a walk, while driving, or during a quiet moment before bedtime.

SHEILA JACOBS

Summer and winter

Let the sea resound, and everything in it, the world, and all who live in it. Let the rivers clap their hands, let the mountains sing together for joy; let them sing before the Lord. (vv. 7–9, NIV)

My favourite time of the year is spring, when everything is fresh and green In this lovely old hymn we are using as the basis of our studies, we read of summer, winter, springtime, and harvest and how every season witnesses to the faithfulness of God. All nature, everything we see, from the magnificence of a starry night to the unique individuality of a snowflake, testifies to a creator, who holds 'all things' together (Hebrews 1:3).

Psalm 24:1 tells us that 'the earth is the Lord's, and everything in it', so how sad it is to see our natural world ruined and destroyed. A brief look at Genesis tells us that in the beginning, when humanity walked in harmony with God, everything was good. Now, like images in shattered pieces of a broken mirror, we still see the reflection of glory in our natural world. Through the brokenness we can detect the hand of our faithful God.

It's often like this in our lives. We have our springtime, summer, autumn, and winter. This isn't necessarily connected to age. Seasons change – some life seasons, such as parenthood, then becoming a grandparent, indicate the natural marching of time. But others – seasons of illness, of sorrow – can also interrupt our lives.

When we're going through times of trouble, it can feel as if that season may never end. When I was ill for several years with Meniere's disease and couldn't work or really do much at all, my mother told me: 'All things pass.' How right she was. I came out of that season of sickness and was able to live a 'normal' life again, praise God – although I was greatly changed by the experience. God can use our brokenness and bring good from it (Romans 8:28). Trust him!

Are you going through a difficult season? Who is supporting you, encouraging you to look to God? Or maybe you are walking with someone else through such a time. Lean into God and praise him for his faithfulness.

SHEILA JACOBS

Pardon for sin

When Jesus saw their faith, he said, 'Friend, your sins are forgiven.' The Pharisees and the teachers of the law began thinking to themselves, 'Who is this fellow who speaks blasphemy? Who can forgive sins but God alone?' (vv. 20–21, NIV)

Who can forgive sins – except God? Here we have Jesus forgiving the sins of the paralysed man and proving his power to do so by healing him too. Jesus is the fullness of God 'in bodily form' (Colossians 2:9), here making that message clear to those – then and now – who question his authority.

Today's passage also includes the call of Levi, who was a tax collector despised by his own people for working with the Roman occupiers of the nation to force money out of the population. Jesus asks Levi to follow him, and he does so – immediately.

In Luke 7 we find another person who has been forgiven – a woman described as 'a sinner' (v. 39), but who is commended by Jesus. Jesus later tells the parable of the two men standing before God – one repentant, the other proud (Luke 18:9–14). The one who knows he is in the wrong says, 'God, have mercy on me, a sinner' (v. 13). Jesus says this is the one who went home 'justified before God' (v. 14).

When I first became a Christian, I'm not sure I really thought I was a sinner! It was only as time went on and I realised I couldn't walk a straight path on my own, and kept veering off, that I recognised how much I had been forgiven and how much I needed the Holy Spirit to warn me, check me, comfort me, and encourage me.

In truth, we are all helpless to save ourselves – as was the thief on the cross who cried out to Jesus and received forgiveness (Luke 23), even though he had never lifted a finger to 'work for God'. Receive forgiveness; then let God work in and through you!

Thank you, Lord, that you have forgiven me! Help me, too, to forgive others – especially where I struggle to do so. Amen.

SHEILA JACOBS

A peace that endureth

For to us a child is born, to us a son is given, and the government will be on his shoulders. And he will be called Wonderful Counsellor, Mighty God, Everlasting Father, Prince of Peace. (v. 6, NIV)

When the angels heralded the birth of Jesus, peace was one of their declarations: 'On earth peace to those on whom his favour rests' (Luke 2:14). His favour surely rests on those who have trusted God's Son, the Prince of Peace, who brings reconciliation between God and humankind.

In our world, there seems to be little peace. Life is tough for many people, and we constantly hear of wars, suffering, and trouble, bringing fear and unrest both internationally and closer to home.

Yet here is Jesus, the 'peace that endureth', able to give us inner stillness in the middle of personal conflict. The peace between God and humanity rests solely in Jesus – the one who gave himself so that we no longer need to be separated from our faithful God.

In the upper room, before Jesus yielded to capture, torture, and death, he gave his first followers a wonderful promise: 'Peace I leave with you; my peace I give you. I do not give to you as the world gives. Do not let your hearts be troubled and do not be afraid' (John 14:27). That's the promise he also gives to you and to me.

Throughout his ministry, Jesus lived a life of peace. He spent a great deal of time seeking out his Father's presence, and his close walk with the Father came from that communion, through the power of the Holy Spirit. Can it really be that we can know the same peace as Jesus had? This isn't a temporary peaceful feeling caused by good circumstances, happy relationships, or a career going well. All these things can change. But the unchanging one gives himself – his very own self – to us, and that's why we need never allow our hearts to be fearful.

Lord, I need your peace today. I believe you promise it to me. Forgive me for letting my heart be afraid, when you have promised me everything I need to be at peace. Amen.

SHEILA JACOBS

Thine own dear presence

'I will ask the Father, and he will give you another advocate to help you and be with you for ever – the Spirit of truth… he lives with you and will be in you'. (vv. 16–17, NIV)

I wonder how it would impact our lives if we really thought about these words spoken by Jesus before he was taken away and crucified.

When Jesus died, then rose again – proving that his sacrifice was accepted by the Father and that every word he ever uttered could be trusted – he told his disciples to wait for the coming of the Spirit, which we read about in the first chapters of the book of Acts. Previously fearful people were suddenly emboldened to tell everyone the good news of Jesus and what he had done for them!

The Spirit of God leads us into truth (John 16:13). He equips us (see 1 Corinthians 12) and helps us to pray when we don't know what to say (Romans 8:26). It is sobering to read, too, that our bodies are his temple, so we need to honour God with them (1 Corinthians 6:19–20).

The Holy Spirit gives us power to live for God. We simply cannot do this on our own. Only God can live the God-life!

It is truly awe-inspiring to read that the same Spirit 'who raised Jesus from the dead is living in [us]' (Romans 8:11). But what does that mean, in our daily lives?

The Holy Spirit makes the presence of God real for us. We have talked in these notes about the relationship we have with God, made possible through Jesus. But the one who makes it a dynamic walk, a power-filled experience, is the Holy Spirit. Ephesians 5:18 urges us to 'be filled with the Spirit', and as we receive that filling, we can overflow to others.

However, sometimes we can become dry, and our God-walk seems to be disconnected in some way. If that sounds like you, maybe it's time to get connected with God's presence again!

Do you need to ask God to fill you with his Holy Spirit today? He is faithful – so ask with faith in him and believe that you have received!

SHEILA JACOBS

Strength, hope and blessings!

In his great mercy he has given us new birth into a living hope through the resurrection of Jesus Christ from the dead, and into an inheritance that can never perish, spoil or fade. This inheritance is kept in heaven for you. (vv. 3–4, NIV)

We come to the final day of this study based on the hymn 'Great is thy faithfulness'. We have been exploring aspects of the faithfulness of God and now come to the epic: 'Strength for today and bright hope for tomorrow, blessings all mine, with ten thousand beside!'

Strength for today – we have God's promise of his presence, given to us through the Holy Spirit. *Bright hope for tomorrow* – because Jesus will never leave us. Even though we travel through a land that is often difficult to navigate, we are on our way to somewhere beautiful, gifted to us through the finished work of Jesus on the cross. *Blessings all mine* – are they just for the future or for today too? We only have to review the past to know the answer. I'm sure you, like me, can see evidence of his blessing along the way. How comforting to know that this faithfulness will continue with us as we step into the future.

Today's passage from 1 Peter incorporates verses given to me when I was baptised. The journey hasn't always been easy, although there have been points of resting, kind surprises, and beautiful views. Looking back, I can see God's equipping and provision, and this gives me hope for tomorrow. I know the faithful one accompanies me.

We are pilgrims, and this world is a temporary home. What we see on earth is just a shadow of things to come – as it says in 1 Corinthians 13:12, 'For now we see through a glass, darkly' (KJV). But it won't always be so. Whether you have walked with Jesus for a long time or have only recently begun the journey, I pray that you will know more of his presence and his faithfulness, today and always.

Lord Jesus, thank you that you give me strength for the day, hope for tomorrow, and blessings. This is all made possible through your sacrifice on the cross, Lord. Thank you for your presence in my life! Amen.

SHEILA JACOBS

Wise words from women in the Bible

Chine McDonald writes…

Have you ever heard it said that women speak 20,000 words a day on average, compared to men who speak just 7,000? This statistic has been dispelled as myth – or at least very difficult to prove – but it speaks to clichés we have about gender differences in communication. Women are characterised as those who speak and express their feelings and emotions with each other, while men are stereotyped as keeping their thoughts and emotions inside.

Meanwhile, the opposite characterisation is also true. I have been at many meetings or gatherings where I mentally clock up the amount of time men are taking up with their words, compared to the women in their midst. This just goes to show that stereotypes are wrong! However, when it comes to the amount of space taken up by men in the Bible, we can be certain that women speak very rarely compared to men. It is thought that women speak 14,046 words in the Bible. While that may sound like a lot, it accounts for just 1.1% of the words in scripture.

Perhaps it is a case of quality over quantity, because in the words of women in scripture we find power, beauty, and wisdom. We also find deep theological insight, emotional depth, and prophetic imagination. For example, the words of Jesus' mother in the Magnificat (Luke 1:46–55) express both humility and revolutionary hope, while Ruth's pledge to Naomi – 'Where you go I will go' (Ruth 1:16) – is a declaration of loyalty and love that transcends cultural boundaries.

Women's speech in the Bible often conveys profound truths on the nature of God. Mary Magdalene is the first to witness the risen Christ at a time when a woman's word counted for little in comparison to a man's. Her testimony reminds us of the God we serve – a God who sees differently than the world does, whose kingdom is not of this earth.

Reflecting on these voices highlights the importance of listening to and valuing women's perspectives in faith communities today. Their words continue to inspire, challenge, and lead, just as they did in biblical times. As you reflect on the wise words of women this week, may you be inspired and reinvigorated to walk in the paths of the mighty women of God who have gone before you.

Hannah: 'There is no rock like our God'

'There is no one holy like the Lord; there is no one besides you; there is no Rock like our God.' (v. 2, NIV)

I have always been astounded by the faithfulness to God exhibited by those who experience profound suffering and pain. In such situations, it feels almost natural to reject the idea of a loving God. Hannah had desperately wanted children with her husband Elkanah. Like many women, she experienced the deep frustration, anxiety, heartbreak, and shame of being unable to conceive and give birth.

In the opening chapter of 1 Samuel, we see Hannah and Elkanah going to the tabernacle at Shiloh to worship and give sacrifices to God. Hannah is in deep distress and anguish, pouring out her prayers to God in a way that the priest Eli does not recognise: silently. Hannah still believes that God will hear her prayer. Rather than turn away from God, she turns towards the holy one.

In today's passage, we see the aftermath of God's fulfilled promises to Hannah. She does not forget what God has done for her but rejoices in the Lord. What we see here is how the miraculous thing that God does in her life turns her outwards rather than inwards. Yes, God has done great things for her personally, but God will do spectacular and unexpected things in the world: breaking the bows of the warriors and lifting those in need from the ash heap. Hannah remains sure that 'there is no rock like our God'.

I find her witness to God's faithfulness inspiring. I know that at times I take my eyes off God's goodness and look to other sources, including myself, to achieve my heart's desires. But today, may we be inspired to be those that sing of God's great goodness, no matter what is happening in our lives.

Loving God, may we always stay close to you – in the ups and downs, the good times and the bad times. Help us to be faithful to you, forever singing of your praises. Amen.

CHINE MCDONALD

Mary: 'He has filled the hungry with good things'

'He has shown strength with his arm; he has scattered the proud in the thoughts of their hearts; he has brought down the mighty from their thrones and exalted those of humble estate; he has filled the hungry with good things, and the rich he has sent away empty.' (vv. 51–53, ESV)

I grew up in a faith tradition that didn't pay very close attention to Jesus' mother Mary. When our eyes were turned towards her, what we heard were stories about her submission in saying yes to God. We heard about her being a doting and loving mother. We heard about her faithfulness. But we rarely heard about her wisdom and her prophetic power.

In today's passage we read Mary's song – also known as the Magnificat. Here, Mary echoes the prophetic song of her foremother Hannah (see yesterday's reading) in singing praise to God, marvelling at who God is and telling of what God can and will do. Mary's Magnificat is gloriously sung in Anglican and Catholic churches all over the world, often set to extraordinarily beautiful music.

Mary's words are not just the chaste warbling of a young woman but paint a powerful and prophetic picture of the new order of God's kingdom, in which the world will be turned right-way-up. A place where the mighty will be pulled down from their thrones, the humble will be exalted, the hungry will be filled with good things, and the rich will be sent away empty.

In the turbulence and chaos of today's world, it is hard to imagine these things. We are so often seeing the opposite – the rich getting richer and military and economic power, strength, and might being seen as the ultimate good. It is among the permacrises that I see around me that Mary's words are so wise and impactful – seeing beyond the immediate surroundings and looking towards what God can and will do.

If you were to write your own version of the Magnificat for today's world, what would the world turned right-way-up look like?

CHINE MCDONALD

Naomi: 'Just be patient... until we hear what happens'

Then Naomi said to her, 'Just be patient, my daughter, until we hear what happens. The man won't rest until he has settled things today.' (v. 18, NLT)

Patience is one of my least practised of the fruit of the Spirit. With life being so fast-paced, I often find myself striving to get things done quickly and get them out of the way. I recognise that I am attempting to exert a sense of control over my surroundings, to take things into my own hand. The thing about patience is that it often requires you to wait for another person to act in some way. It usually involves relinquishing control.

In today's passage, Naomi demonstrates patience in waiting for God's provision. Despite the great loss she suffered, she did not act impulsively. Instead, she wisely guided Ruth in how to approach Boaz and trusted that he would be able to secure their future.

Ruth also showed remarkable patience and obedience and submitted to her mother-in-law's instruction. She had to wait until Boaz had finished eating and drinking before approaching him as he slept. Ruth had to patiently wait for his response. Boaz did not rush to claim Ruth but first sought to do what was right and see if another relative had the first right to redeem her. The events of Ruth 3 teach the importance of patience in waiting for God's plan to unfold.

Ruth and Naomi did not manipulate circumstances but trusted God's provision. Their patience led to a greater reward – Ruth's eventual marriage to Boaz and her place in Jesus' family line. Their story reminds us that patience, faith, and wise action bring about God's perfect timing. Spirit-filled patience requires us to surrender our need to take things into our own hands and trust that God is the one in control.

Loving God, thank you that nothing is a surprise to you. Help us to lay down our worries and anxieties about the future today and trust wholeheartedly in your will and love for us. Amen.

CHINE MCDONALD

Abigail: 'Let me take the blame!'

As soon as Abigail saw David, she got off her donkey and fell on her knees at his feet, her face to the ground in homage, saying, 'My master, let me take the blame! Let me speak to you. Listen to what I have to say.' (vv. 23–24, MSG)

Can you think of a time when you have had to take the blame for someone else's bad behaviour? It is an extremely challenging thing to do, especially if, like me, you value being seen as a good, upstanding, moral person. However, sometimes good and wise leadership requires the humility of taking the blame for things that we have not done. But it is not easy – neither in a home or a work context.

This is one of the things that makes Abigail's story so remarkable. As the wife of Nabal, a wealthy but harsh and foolish man who brings danger to their family by refusing to give provisions to King David and his men when they ask, Abigail knows that she must intervene to avoid catastrophe on her household. She thinks clearly and quickly, gathering food and supplies, and taking the initiative to go and speak to David directly, telling him to let her take the blame for what Nabal did.

I find it much easier to take responsibility for my children's bad behaviour – I want to protect them – but taking the blame for what another adult has done would require me to grit my teeth and muster up the humility to be seen as the one in the wrong. Abigail not only did this but also demonstrated wisdom and diplomacy, reminding David of his divine calling and urging him not to shed innocent blood in anger. As a result, David praised her wisdom, and later, after Nabal's death, she became David's wife. Her story serves as an enduring lesson in how taking responsibility can lead to peace, prevent disaster, and align us with God's greater plans.

Gracious God, help us to be humble in all we do. Help us lay down our need to be seen as right, as good, or as those who please people. Help us to have the courage to seek your divine will, even when it costs us. In Jesus' name. Amen.

CHINE MCDONALD

Mary: 'Do whatever he tells you'

'Woman, why do you involve me?' Jesus replied. 'My hour has not yet come.' His mother said to the servants, 'Do whatever he tells you'. (vv. 4–5, NIV)

The wedding at Cana is one of the rare occasions when Jesus' mother is described as being present to witness her Son's miracle. So often Mary is depicted as having a passive role in the early church, but her active role in this story is closer to how historical accounts have described her. In ancient depictions of the early church, Mary is often featured as a leader in the Jesus movement, illustrated as a prophetic figure with her arms outstretched above her head as some of the great biblical heroes are often imagined.

In today's passage, we see Mary taking the lead and telling those gathered behind the scenes at the wedding to do as Jesus says. Mary's deep faith, trust, and obedience is seen in this story. She is Jesus' mother, yes, but she is also his disciple. As a mother of sons, I can imagine that in such a situation I would want to tell my boys what they should do and how they should do it. Mary, however, does not instruct Jesus, but entrusts the situation to him, confident in his wisdom and power. Her words to the servants encourage them – and us – to surrender completely to Christ's will.

By following Jesus' instructions to fill the jars with water, the servants take part in the first recorded miracle, the transformation of water into wine. This act illustrates how obedience to Christ, even when we're not sure of what might come next or unsure of the task required of us, can lead to miraculous and truly awesome results.

Mary's words also remind us that faith requires action. It is not enough to hear Jesus' words; we are required to do something.

Wonderful God, thank you for the beauty of being in relationship with you. Thank you that we can hear from you. Help us to have the faith and courage to do what you tell us to do, in every situation. Amen.

CHINE MCDONALD

Rebekah: 'Yes, I will go'

Then they said, 'Let's call the young woman and ask her about it.' So they called Rebekah and asked her, 'Will you go with this man?' 'I will go,' she said. (vv. 57–58, NIV)

Many years ago, I was in a job I loved, working on a local newspaper. I had joined just after the credit crunch had hit, and the paper lost a lot in advertising revenue as businesses struggled. One day we were called into a room and told by the boss that cuts would have to be made and that we would start with voluntary redundancies. As soon as he said the words, I heard what felt like the audible voice of God in my ear: 'You can go.' It was one of the times I can say that I heard God most vividly and clearly.

However, it was not something I would have wanted or chosen to do. I was in a safe and secure position in a place I loved. I couldn't guarantee what would come next. But I was obedient to that voice of God and took voluntary redundancy. That step of obedience was the first step into a career that has turned out to be more than I could have hoped or wished for.

In today's passage, Rebekah's willingness to go reflects her deep faith, courage, and trust. She had never met Isaac, yet she trusted that this journey was part of something greater. Her decision mirrors other biblical figures, like Abraham, who also obeyed God's call without knowing all the details.

Rebekah's story challenges us to consider our own readiness to follow God's plan, even when it requires stepping into the unknown. Are we willing to leave our comfort zones, trusting that God's guidance is enough? Like Rebekah, we too may be called to listen to God, trust and bravely say: 'I will go.' If we believe that God's path is good, then what could we possibly be worried about?

Loving God, thank you for the adventure of faith that you call us into. Help us to trust in your call on our lives, even when we don't know where the next steps will lead. Amen.

CHINE MCDONALD

Lydia: 'Come and stay at my house'

When she and the members of her household were baptised, she invited us to her home. 'If you consider me a believer in the Lord,' she said, 'come and stay at my house.' And she persuaded us. (v. 15, NIV)

I feel most fully alive when I am cooking for friends and family and having everyone tuck into a sumptuous meal. There is something profoundly beautiful about meeting around a table with friends old and new under one roof. I imagine the earliest Christian communities spent a lot of time eating together.

The book of Acts is full of tales of encounter and adventure among the earliest followers of Jesus. They must have seen wonders, and they must have excitedly shared what they had seen God do among their friends and family, but also the wider community that was being drawn towards the gospel of Jesus Christ. These Jesus followers needed those who could provide space for them to gather and rest and would have relied on the hospitality of those who had homes and means.

I love that the Bible includes stories of women like Lydia, who did not necessarily conform to the standards and norms of womanhood at the time. It is remarkable that when they arrived in Macedonia, Paul and his followers sat down with a group of women. Women were very much included in this new community with Christ Jesus as its cornerstone, and women like Lydia did the including themselves. A recent convert, she was a woman of means – a dealer in purple cloth – who was able to open her home to Paul and his entourage.

Some of us may believe we do not have much to give or much to add to the mission of God, but Lydia's wisdom in opening her home showed that she saw herself as able to make a contribution, even if it was in a different way to others.

Generous God, may we recognise what we can uniquely bring to you. Help us to hear your voice and discern what you are calling us to do. Amen.

CHINE MCDONALD

The significance and symbolism of wells in the Bible

Jenny Sanders writes…

When I was growing up, one of our neighbours had an ornamental well in her front garden. It struck me as a whimsical thing more suited to the world of fairy tales. There was certainly a clear resemblance between her garden fixture and the illustrations in Jack and Jill from our nursery rhyme book: a gabled, red-tiled roof atop a circular wall of stones and, in the space between, a bucket fixed to a pulley, complete with a handle for winding.

In the UK, we simply turn on the tap to access water. A temperate climate with high rainfall makes everything flourish: green fields, lush pastures, and sturdy trees. Gardens prosper and footpaths become overgrown, impeding progress for walkers, despite carefully navigating nettles and brambles. Even in times of drought, when we're urged to save water, take showers rather than baths, and obey the hosepipe bans, we know that autumn and winter will come soon enough. We're complacent about the luxury of hot and cold running water in our homes, but before the invention of indoor plumbing, wells were the major water source for everyone.

In biblical times, wells were significantly less pretty than that of our neighbour but were far more useful. Where the landscape was mostly desert – rocky, arid, and challenging – communities relied on hard labour to dig deep into the unforgiving earth to reach below the water table where vital, life-sustaining water could be found for people, livestock, and crops.

The Hebrew words for well suggest two different types. *Be'er* would be the most familiar to us. This is an artificial pit, dug deeply enough to access an underground water source and accumulate it. A *bor* refers to a man-made cistern where rainwater could be collected and stored. Both Joseph and Jeremiah were incarcerated in cisterns for a while. While modern wells can be drilled rather than dug and accessed with a pump mechanism instead of the laborious use of a rope and bucket, the principle hasn't changed at all.

Over the next fortnight we'll be visiting some biblical wells, loitering at the community meeting place and enjoying their symbolism as places of blessing and provision.

Hagar's wells

Then God opened her eyes and she saw a well of water. (21:19, NIV)

Life without water is unsustainable – one of the reasons why life on planet earth can flourish is because of the presence of water. Hagar didn't have any scientific knowledge, but she knew that without water she and her son would both die. She experienced the painful prospect of dying of thirst not once, but twice.

In today's passage, she runs away from Sarah and Abraham's camp, having slept with her master (her mistress' misguided idea), fallen pregnant and, while unwisely despising her barren boss, struggled with her subsequent mistreatment to the point of despair. We see her have an interaction with an angel in the Sinai desert, who not only directs her to go back home, but also promises her a blessed future and a son. He reassures her that God has heard her and seen her. Consequently, the well by which she'd camped was given a name that meant 'Well of the Living One who sees me' – Beer Lahai Roi.

Five chapters and several years later, once the child of promise, Isaac, was born, Hagar and Ishmael were sent away permanently. This time she was sure they would die until God, who had heard Ishmael weeping, intervened: 'Then God opened her eyes and she saw a well of water. So she went and filled the skin with water and gave the boy a drink' (21:19). God's provision was already there.

Sometimes we can't see for looking. When the walls press in and we're so taken up with our circumstances that we become the centre of our world, it's all too easy to miss God's provision. Hagar almost did. This well was, quite literally, a lifesaver – provided at just the right time and in just the right place.

I wonder if you need to lift your head today to discover God's provision for you.

Think about your most immediate and pressing circumstances. Ask yourself whether they have temporarily obscured your view of God. Invite the Holy Spirit to open your ears and eyes as you encounter him today.

JENNY SANDERS

Abraham's well

'Accept these seven lambs from my hand as a witness that I dug this well.' (v. 30, NIV)

Around the time that Isaac was born, a quarrel broke out between the households of Abraham and Abimelek over ownership of a well. The previous chapter explains how Abraham had been living in an area under King Abimelek's jurisdiction. There had been conflict between them since the king took Sarah under his care, believing that she was Abraham's sister, not his wife. That lie, if perpetuated, could have ruined God's plan and covenant promise given in chapters 12 and 15.

Abimelek's servants falsely claimed the well was theirs, which avoided the strenuous work of digging their own and indicates some jealousy over Abraham's flourishing flocks and herds. Their master claimed ignorance of the matter, but Abraham initiated a treaty to settle the argument and usher in a time of peace. A deal was made and sealed by setting apart seven ewe lambs from Abraham's flocks. These are the most valuable since they carry the reproductive value of a flock, remaining fertile for a good seven to ten years.

Seven has always been regarded as the biblical number of completeness and perfection, appearing many times throughout the Bible, including the seven days of creation.

Abraham's lambs foreshadow the lamb of God who, in his perfect holiness, has brought peace between God and humanity through his sacrificial death, resurrection, and ascension. Abimelek chose to accept the lambs. We also have a choice to make regarding accepting *the* lamb. The fact that you are reading these notes indicates you've probably already made that choice, but it's one we can make each day.

Abraham's well, or the 'well of seven', still stands in Beersheba. Verse 33 says that 'there [Abraham] called on the name of the Lord, the Eternal God'. What a wonderful example of connecting us with God our Father and Jesus our peace.

Thank God for Jesus, who 'himself is our peace, who… has destroyed the barrier, the dividing wall of hostility' between us and sealed the 'treaty' with his precious blood (Ephesians 2:14).

JENNY SANDERS

Rebekah's well

Before he had finished praying, Rebekah came out with her jar on her shoulder... Then the man bowed down and worshipped the Lord. (vv. 15, 26, NIV)

This is the start of a beautiful love story that began by a well. (Read to the end of the chapter to discover the outcome.) We've called this 'Rebekah's well', but the focus is on Abraham's servant, who couldn't bring himself to call on God from his own meagre measure of faith but relied on that of his master. He was richly rewarded with an answer before he'd even finished praying.

On a quest to find a suitable wife for Isaac, the child of promise, now a grown man, the servant was under strict instructions not to look for a candidate among the Canaanites or Chaldeans. He sets off to the land that Abraham came from. They were already in the land that God had promised.

Although that promise wouldn't be fulfilled for many years, Abraham's specifications expressed his conviction that God would be faithful to prepare an unknown, unseen bride. She would be a living testimony to the covenant promise – a deposit of that which was still to come.

Perhaps the servant wobbled – his only assurance the claim that God's angel would go ahead of him and ensure success (v. 40). In his simple prayer by the town well, he called out to Abraham's God.

What grace that before he'd even completed his prayer, God answered. In the cool of the day, Rebekah arrived to draw water for her family and responded positively to the man's bold request. Camels can drink up to 32 gallons (145 litres) of water in one watering. With ten to satiate, it must have taken considerable time and effort to haul enough water for them all.

Verse 26 sees the man worshipping God for himself and thanking God for providentially leading him to Abraham's relatives. Rebekah's family received him (and his gifts) warmly. A new chapter had begun.

Thank you, Father God, that you often answer my prayers before I've even uttered them. I am so grateful for your faithfulness, your presence, your provision, and your promises. Amen.

JENNY SANDERS

Blocked wells

So all the wells that his father's servants had dug in the time of his father Abraham, the Philistines stopped up, filling them with earth. (v. 15, NIV)

Whoever owned the wells – or had access to the supply of water – held both power and control. Isaac had grown so wealthy that he was now considered a threat by the Philistines, who retaliated by sabotaging the wells his father had used. Using stones, wood, rubbish, even dead animals, they effectively plugged the lifeline, hoping to force him away, to give up the land he occupied and the pastures he used. This was an effective strategy often used by Israel's enemies. 2 Kings 3:25 records how the Midianites destroyed towns, fields, and blocked wells in Elisha's day.

If fresh water symbolises the living water of life in Christ, a stopped-up well stands for a cutting off or interruption of resources which must bring spiritual death. What impedes the flow of fresh Holy Spirit 'water' into our lives?

Perhaps we've neglected our relationship with Jesus. Relationships require time and effort if they're to flourish but also to endure through challenging seasons. Maybe we've compromised somewhere at home or at work in what we've chosen to read, hear, or watch and are finding it difficult to hear God's voice.

It could be that a crisis has occurred – medical or financial – a bereavement or a betrayal of trust which has thrown us off kilter. Instead of living in a place of peace, we can find ourselves overwhelmed with anxiety and doubt as we retreat from God instead of run towards him.

Remember, it's our enemy, Satan, who seeks to 'steal and kill and destroy' (John 10:10), our trust, our hope, our joy, our assurance, even our faith. He loves to see us disempowered, cut off from our loving heavenly Father. Peter encourages us to be alert to the devil's schemes and resist him with all our might (1 Peter 5:8–9).

Can you identify wells in your life which have become blocked recently? Take some time to bring this before God and pray for his wisdom and insight. Let today be the day they are unblocked.

JENNY SANDERS

Reopening the wells

Isaac reopened the wells that had been dug in the time of his father Abraham, which the Philistines had stopped up after Abraham died, and he gave them the same names his father had given them.
(v. 18, NIV)

If Isaac hadn't believed that there was still water in the old wells, he wouldn't have bothered to reopen them. Having been instructed by King Abimelek to move on, he relocated to a valley – often symbolic of a place of trial and suffering. His father's wells were not only reopened but given their original names – a mark of ownership, value, and respect.

Isaac's men found new water sources and dug two wells, but their ownership was contested. Finally, a third well went unchallenged.

Isaac's perseverance led to an encounter with God in which the promise his father had carried in his heart was reiterated. 'That night the Lord appeared to [Isaac] and said: "I am the God of your father Abraham. Do not be afraid, for I am with you; I will bless you and will increase the number of your descendants for the sake of my servant Abraham"' (26:24). It's the first time we see Isaac build an altar where he 'called on the name of the Lord' (v. 25) for himself.

God blesses families of believers. The plan has always been that God's life, God's words, and God's promises would pass on from one generation to another. There's a sense of overflow, of passing on a baton of faith from the older to the younger, a continuation of the walk with God that illustrates the solidity and consistency of his enduring promises. The Abrahamic covenant was for all generations, which includes us (Genesis 17:7). By utilising the same names of the wells that his father had used, Isaac acknowledged Abraham's close walk with God.

Whether you're a first-generation Jesus-follower or a thirty-first one, God's promises and his living water are just as available as they ever have been. Wells that were closed off can be reopened.

Lord Jesus, you are the water of life. Thank you for those who have prayed for your blessing over me. Give me a fresh flow of your Spirit today as I focus on you again. Help me to hear you clearly. Amen.

JENNY SANDERS

Rachel's well

When Jacob saw Rachel daughter of his uncle Laban, and Laban's sheep, he went over and rolled the stone away from the mouth of the well and watered his uncle's sheep. (v. 10, NIV)

In Genesis 28, Jacob had his famous dream of a ladder and heard God repeat the covenantal promise given to his father and grandfather, alongside a promise of protection. Bearing in mind he was really running away from the wrath of his brother and the disappointment of his father, who he had deceived to steal the family blessing, this was a pivotal moment. Jacob declared that if God kept his promises to give him safety and success, he would worship him himself.

In today's reading, providentially, he arrived in his wider family's locale. There are echoes of the encounter Abraham's servant had with Rebekah at another well.

When cousin Rachel arrived with her sheep, Jacob came to the rescue. Rather than wait until all the flocks were gathered, as was the custom, he removed the covering stone so that her sheep could drink immediately. The stone emphasised ownership, protected it from excessive evaporation and vandals, and prevented accidents. Perhaps Jacob also wanted to show off his strength in front of the girl he fell for so fast. Rachel's name means 'ewe' and, in a sense, Jacob foreshadows Jesus providing for his flock (us).

In many ways the story of Jacob and Rachel is a love story. Despite tricky Uncle Laban cunningly marrying him off to his elder daughter, Leah, after seven years of service, Jacob gladly worked another seven for the girl he truly loved (Genesis 29:20). It is also a tale of heartache and jealousy between siblings and children (Genesis 30:1; 37:3), but it was a vital steppingstone in God's plan to ensure his man, Joseph, would be in Egypt at the right time.

In God's salvation plan, Jacob became Israel, the father of the twelve tribes: the sons of promise.

Thank you, Father God that your plans and purposes are still being worked out today. Help me to walk in step with you and resist jealousies and conflicts that draw me away from you. Amen.

JENNY SANDERS

Moses' well

When Pharaoh heard of this, he tried to kill Moses, but Moses fled from Pharaoh and went to live in Midian, where he sat down by a well. (v. 15, NIV)

Moses' escape from a furious Pharaoh into the land of Midian is marked by yet another encounter at a well. Fearful and on the run, Moses must have been mightily relieved to leave Egypt behind and to find a well which offered refreshment and replenishment. Here, Moses distinguished himself by rescuing seven sisters who came to draw water, from some shepherd bullies who appear to have wanted priority access to the water for their own flocks. He not only stood up for them but also drew the water himself. No wonder the girl's father was horrified to discover he had been left at the well without traditional hospitality.

Here, in obscurity, Moses married Zipporah, one of the daughters of Ruel (later called Jethro), and they had two sons, Gershom and Eliezer. His father-in-law was a priest, and so Moses was put to work as a shepherd while also learning about priesthood. It was another training ground for stepping into the plan and destiny God had for him.

Midian was a turning point for Moses. After 40 years in the palace, learning to be a prince/king, God placed him in a family where he would learn to be a priest for another 40 years. It was all preparation for leading the Jewish people out of slavery and across the Judean wilderness towards the promised land – another 40 years as a prophet.

Moses learned how to be a prophet, priest, and king and so served as a forerunner of Jesus himself.

His story reminds us that nothing in our lives is wasted. Seasons of preparation are vital if we are to fulfil God's plans for us. Our temptation is to rush ahead, but savouring each day and nurturing our relationship and intimacy with him is as refreshing and replenishing as that cool well water was for Moses.

Thank you, Father God, that you know the good plans you have for me. Help me to rest in you, engaging with each step of the preparation and journey you're leading me on, full of faith and patience. Amen.

JENNY SANDERS

Ancient wells

'You gave them kingdoms and nations… they took possession of houses filled with all kinds of good things, wells already dug, vineyards, olive groves and fruit trees in abundance. They ate to the full and were well-nourished; they revelled in your great goodness.' (Nehemiah 9:22, 25, NIV)

Today's reading contains a warning from Moses for the people of Israel as they approached the promised land and a recollection from the prophet Nehemiah who lived more than 800 years later. He reminded the exiles – now returned to Jerusalem and celebrating the completion of the city walls – of God's faithfulness in providing for their forefathers on the journey from Egypt under Moses and then Joshua.

Considering wells as symbolic of God's blessing, we can explore the history of God's power and presence here in the UK. The gospel first came to the UK through godly Roman merchants and then through St Augustine in the southeast, Bishop Aidan in Northumbria (Lindisfarne), St Patrick in Ireland, and St Columba in Scotland (Iona). Communities of monks worked to bring the good news of Jesus to their communities for many years.

History chronicles the ebb and flow of powerful moves of God, of which the 18th-century revivals under John Wesley and George Whitfield and the Welsh revival in the early 20th century are probably the most well-known.

For 20 years we ministered in a Hampshire town where Hudson Taylor had once visited. The seeds of the gospel had been sown many years before we arrived, thanks to godly folk who established an iron foundry, workers' accommodation, a Sunday school, a school, and a church. I am convinced that we benefitted from all that had gone before as we sought God for the community of our generation.

Ancient spiritual wells can still flow with spiritual life, even if we have to dig to reveal it. You may have heard of 'thin places', such as Lindisfarne, where the gap between heaven and earth seems narrow and God's presence is palpable. I wonder what heritage lies dormant in your town.

Embark on some research in your town/city. Is there a spiritual heritage of past moves of God that your community can, by faith, plug into again? Perhaps there are specific ways he has changed lives, which may flow again.

JENNY SANDERS

The well of sorrow

'Very truly I tell you, you will weep and mourn while the world rejoices. You will grieve, but your grief will turn to joy.' (John 16:20, NIV)

The book of Psalms contains many laments, poetic expressions of a feeling of loss, grief, abandonment, or confusion. Each is a heart cry of sorrow that questions God, lays out a particular complaint or situation, and appeals to God's character and promises with a longing that such seasons would end swiftly. Lament played a significant part in the rubric of the early church fathers. It's a healthy, godly way of navigating the darker times of our lives.

Ecclesiastes tells us that there is 'a time to weep and a time to laugh, a time to mourn and a time to dance' (3:4). In the sermon on the mount, Jesus taught: 'Blessed are those who mourn, for they will be comforted' (Matthew 5:4). There is something cathartic about acknowledging our sorrows and hurts. It's a healthy and important part of our healing process our journey to recovery and wholeness. Remember that Jesus himself was 'a man of sorrows, and acquainted with grief' (Isaiah 53:3, ESV).

We may find that sorrow and joy sometimes live side-by-side; and while Jesus was familiar with the pain of sorrow, he was also anointed 'with the oil of joy' (Psalm 45:7).

We can move on too quickly from difficult times. By ignoring or diminishing their impact on us we may find that, like a splinter that's left unattended, they become infected and, in time, cause us further emotional and spiritual pain. Likewise, we can linger at our personal well of sorrow for too long, continually pressing our emotional bruises or picking at the emotional scab, like a child who delays healing.

Sorrow has its place; suffering is inevitable. It can be redemptive when we allow Jesus to fill it, but let's not settle by this particular well.

Lord Jesus, thank you that in your humanity you experienced all the sorrows that I encounter, and more. Holy Spirit, please help me to process my hurts in a way that brings healing to my heart and glory to God. Amen.

JENNY SANDERS

The well of salvation

'The Lord, the Lord himself, is my strength and my defence; he has become my salvation.' With joy you will draw water from the wells of salvation. (vv. 2–3, NIV)

Do you sometimes feel as though your days are interchangeable, each identical to the one before? Dreary days leech the joy from life and can leave us jaded, weary, and depressed. Regardless of how long you've been following Jesus, the wonder of salvation can lose some of its sparkle thanks to the wear and tear of life.

The prophet Isaiah lived about 700 years before Jesus, but his rich prophecies point forward to the coming of the Messiah, God's promised Saviour. His words serve to remind us that connecting with God and the gospel message, which came through Jesus' life, death, resurrection, and ascension, has saved us from sin and death and hell. Truly, a cause for celebration! Returning our focus to him – our life-giving source – provides us with more spiritual water flowing from the well of salvation for us to enjoy in all its fullness.

Another translation for 'defence' in verse 2 is 'song'. Zephaniah 3:17 says that God will 'rejoice over you with singing'. What might that sound like? The lyrics are beyond our imagination. One day we may hear them. The TLV says, 'He will dance for joy over you with singing.' Can you imagine God dancing? What a wonderful image! The passage indicates that we are invited into that expression of unadulterated joy – a noisy whirling, twirling, expression of utter delight.

In Isaiah 55, we're invited to come and drink deeply from God's waters. Nothing will satisfy the deep spiritual thirst inside us like the living waters of salvation. Knowing that we can stand confident and clean before God because of Jesus is a truth that sets us free from our past, brings us peace in the present, and gives us faith for the future.

Let's return to that well and join the heavenly celebration!

Use David's heartfelt prayer if you're feeling spiritually dry today: 'Restore to me the joy of your salvation and grant me a willing spirit, to sustain me' (Psalm 51:12). Amen.

JENNY SANDERS

Prophetic wells

'My people have committed two sins: They have forsaken me, the spring of living water, and have dug their own cisterns, broken cisterns that cannot hold water.' (v. 13, NIV)

Known as 'the weeping prophet', Jeremiah was given the unenviable task of bringing God's word to the kingdom of Judah, warning them that exile lay ahead unless they repented and turned back to God. However, he was also cautioned that the people would not listen to him. What a thankless task, and yet it was one that he undertook out of obedience rather than preference.

God's accusation against his people uses the language of poetry and metaphor. Not only had the people forgotten or ignored God, choosing instead to make their own gods; they also, by turning away from the truths their ancestors knew, had left a generation that persisted in pursuing false gods. These foreign deities were 'broken cisterns' – they promised much but delivered little; they brought no life or joy, just a slide into self-indulgence. The people were forsaking the values of Yahweh and trampling their history and God's reputation in the mud, and it broke God's heart.

Despite sending a string of prophets who urged the Jewish people to return to God and his ways, drastic intervention was the only thing that would eventually shake them out of their spiritual stupor.

Jerusalem is is described as pouring out her sin like water, flaunting her disobedience. I wonder how Jeremiah would describe our cities. He says clearly that Babylon will soon come and conquer the land and its people. God would use the powerful enemy nation to chastise his people before turning his attention to Babylon. There would be consequences for all so that righteousness could flourish once again.

Our own nation has also strayed far from God's intention. Let's remember the words of 2 Chronicles 7:14 (below), pray them, and live them, for the sake of all those we love, so that God's name would be honoured again.

'If my people, who are called by my name, will humble themselves and pray and seek my face and turn from their wicked ways, then I will hear from heaven, and I will forgive their sin and will heal their land.'

JENNY SANDERS

The woman at Jacob's well

'If you knew the gift of God and who it is that asks you for a drink, you would have asked him and he would have given you living water.' 'Sir,' the woman said, 'you have nothing to draw with and the well is deep. Where can you get this living water?' (vv. 10–11, NIV)

This unnamed Samaritan woman lived among the relentless gossip of her town. A colourful past and immoral present combined to compel her to use the well in the heat of the day, avoiding painful stares and pointing fingers where the community gathered. Whether living in the shadows or summoning her courage and defiantly stepping out of her house, she would not forget that five times the men in her life had either rejected her or died. Her self-esteem must have been at rock bottom; her opinion of men in general, low.

Almost 2,000 years after Jacob and his sons dug the well in the region of Shechem, near Mount Gerizim, for their own use, Jesus chose it as the perfect place to bring good news to this woman, lost in the mess of her own life history. As one of the patriarchs and father to the twelve tribes of Israel, Jacob's well held great significance.

Jesus knew she was coming. This was a divine appointment that didn't require an audience of disgruntled disciples. His humanity shines through in his tiredness, but his divinity is evident in his insightful replies to her questions.

I wonder if she hesitated when she saw a Jewish man by the well. His request for a drink led to Holy Spirit-inspired questions that penetrated her carapace of self-protection and gently drew out her honesty. Her initial reluctance was replaced by a desire to share the good news with the whole town regardless of what they thought of her.

In many places, Jesus told people to keep quiet about him and/or their encounters and healings, but on this occasion he revealed himself as the Messiah: the promised one, the hope of Israel, redeemer, and Saviour.

Jacob's well provided a cool drink of salvation, savoured by many.

Loving Father, you know all the details of my past and my present and still love me fiercely. I can't hide from you but long for healing in my deepest parts. Thank you that your living water brings just that. Amen.

JENNY SANDERS

Everlasting, thirst-quenching

'Let anyone who is thirsty come to me and drink. Whoever believes in me, as Scripture has said, rivers of living water will flow from within them.' (vv. 37–38, NIV)

When Jesus stood up in Jerusalem and made this announcement, controversy quickly followed. He claimed to be a well, spring, or fountain of spiritual life. Some people understood; others were confused; the religious elite were furious and jealous. It was a radical claim. From anyone else it would have been blasphemous.

Jesus offered real, spiritually thirst-quenching, abundant, unlimited life. His words ring out with the same truth today. We may look to other 'water' sources for soul satisfaction – work, exercise, family, fitness, travel, food, TV series, etc. – but none of those provide enduring contentment and joy. They're a temporary distraction from our present reality, a pleasant diversion from the challenges that demand our attention, but they cannot bring us the peace that comes from knowing we are accepted, loved, forgiven, and pursued by our heavenly Father, who created us for purpose but in whose eyes we always carry significance simply because we are his children. The prophet Isaiah questions why anyone would look elsewhere (effectively digging their own well) when God offers us himself (Isaiah 55).

In Jesus' words we find the promise that his life not only flows to us from him but will flow from us to others by the power of the Holy Spirit, often symbolised by water in the Bible. We can't live an authentic Christian life by our own efforts. We are in a growing, maturing, intimate relationship with God who sent his Spirit after Jesus' ascension. He is no longer bound by geography but can be with all of us, wherever we are, all of the time.

When we are filled daily with the power and presence of the Hoy Spirit, we carry his life – that living water – inside us and have the opportunity to spill that out on those around us every day.

Father God, please forgive me for times when I've tried to dig my own well to satisfy my spiritual thirst. I know you are the source my heart longs for. Holy Spirit, please fill me afresh today. Amen.

JENNY SANDERS

A glimpse of heaven

'For the Lamb at the centre of the throne will be their shepherd; "he will lead them to springs of living water." "And God will wipe away every tear from their eyes."' (Revelation 7:17, NIV)

The words of Isaiah look forward to the day God will bless his people again after a period of chastisement. Predicted as a time of freedom for captives, of comfort and plenty, the passage expresses God's heart for his people, a promise that he will never forget them – their very names are written on his hands. The scars of Jesus somehow carry our names too.

Verse 10 says he 'will lead them beside springs of water'. Whether these are natural springs bubbling up in man-made wells or tumbling straight out of a hillside, God reassures his people that he will ensure their access to spiritual water of refreshment, restoration, and replenishment.

The prophecy is echoed in John's words in Revelation. The final book of the Bible is full of astonishing visions, apocalyptic pictures, and strange creatures, but the clear message is that the victory Jesus won through the cross and resurrection will one day be fully ratified in heaven, as earthly history ends. Whatever turbulent times must still be navigated on earth, the outcome is certain: Jesus wins; God's throne is established; it will not, cannot, fall.

The focus of heaven is the worship of God – not some interminable Sunday service or harp-playing monotony, but a celebration beyond our wildest dreams, full of countless angels and saints. We will finally understand who we are and, more importantly, know fully who he is and what he has accomplished. Sorrow, sickness, and death will be banished forever – the shadow of a dream – and we will be led again to 'streams of living water'. There we'll be able to drink deeply in, and of, his company. No more clock-watching. No more anxiety. No more man-made programmes. Just a glorious, eternal intimacy where our focus will be fully taken up with our wonderful Saviour.

Glorious Father, thank you for the promise of heaven, and for reminding me that you are in control and working your purposes out. Help me to drink deeply and regularly from your wonderful wells of salvation life. Amen.

JENNY SANDERS

Lord, teach us to pray

Sara Batts-Neale writes…

In the next two weeks we will explore prayer with Jesus. We will be asking him every day to teach us to pray, just as his disciples did. I wonder how old you were when you learned the Lord's Prayer. I think I've always known it – although at some point I must have been taught the words. I have probably said it thousands of times in my lifetime, from primary school to ordination and beyond.

It's a bit different from the early church, where you weren't taught the Lord's Prayer until after you'd been baptised and the whole ritual of initiation at baptism was dramatically different. We know this from the writings of a fourth-century bishop, Cyril of Jerusalem, and we'll consider some of his thoughts in the next few days. I do find myself wondering if we have lost something of the power of this prayer by its very ubiquity. How would we relate to the words if we prayed them only annually, or monthly, rather than daily? What if we said them so carefully there could be no misunderstandings? (God's name is not Harold, and it's not the words of Jesus' tortoise…)

Let's do that, slowing down over the next fortnight. In the first week, we'll look at some of the times Jesus prayed and his teachings about prayer, perseverance, hope, and trust. We will think about where and how Jesus prayed, from his baptism to the garden at Gethsemane. Our Bible passages will be mainly from Luke, since Luke puts such an emphasis on prayer, but we will also visit Matthew and Mark for their ideas, along with other passages. In the second week, we'll focus on the words Jesus taught us, reflecting line-by-line on how the prayer centres our faith.

In teaching us to pray, Jesus teaches us about our relationship with God and with others. He tells us what we can expect, and he reminds us that our prayers do not need to be all-singing, all-dancing affairs. In my tradition prayers are short and to the point – I'm a great believer in the advice in Matthew 6:7 – but your prayers may be longer or more conversational. What matters is that we do pray – that we acknowledge our dependence on, and give thanks, praise, and glory to, our heavenly Father.

Jesus prays at his baptism

Now when all the people were baptised and when Jesus also had been baptised and was praying, the heaven was opened. (v. 21, NRSV)

A baptism is such a joyful thing. Whether it's an adult being baptised as a testimony to a new-found faith or an infant brought by parents, it is a cause for celebration. In my opinion it's one of the best things a minister is able to do. In the Church of England's liturgy, we pray for the Spirit to guide and strengthen us as God's faithful people. We trust that the Holy Spirit will daily renew us as pilgrim people. We pray – just as Jesus did at his own baptism.

Our passage today takes us to the start of Jesus' adult ministry. Luke tells us here that Jesus was praying at his baptism. Luke has set the scene with the time and the place – John the Baptist's prophetic work is well underway, with crowds coming to him for baptism and to hear his words of wisdom. Without ceremony, Jesus' baptism takes place. He's last in the queue after all the other people.

In Luke's account, Jesus prays after his baptism and the Holy Spirit descends in the form of a dove. Right at the start of Jesus' ministry, he prays. I'd love to know what that prayer was – how amazing it would be to be able to use more of Jesus' words at our own baptism services! I'd also love to be able to see the Holy Spirit – to be completely assured my prayer for the Spirit had been answered. I'd rather not be led into the desert for 40 days, though.

Jesus teaches us to pray as we begin a new venture. He reminds us that we too can rely on the Holy Spirit, who guides and strengthens us not just on the day of our baptism but throughout our lives as we follow him through life's temptations.

'Trust in the Lord forever, for the Lord, the Lord himself, is the Rock eternal' (Isaiah 26:4, NIV).

SARA BATTS-NEALE

Jesus prays for the apostles

During those days [Jesus] went out to the mountain to pray, and he spent the night in prayer to God. (v. 12, NRSV)

Jesus teaches us today to pray before making a major choice. What kind of big decisions have you made in your life? Finding new jobs, deciding to marry or end a relationship, new homes – these are all things that shape our lives. I'm writing this while waiting for a house move to be finalised. This uncertainty currently features rather heavily in my prayer life! Like yesterday's wish for a visible Spirit, I find myself wishing God would provide rather more obvious signs. Often, it's easier to spot where God was at work in hindsight than in the moment. I will also confess that sometimes I am guilty of bringing a decision to God and hoping he will rubber stamp it, rather than truly being open to where God might point.

Jesus' ministry is well underway by this point in Luke's gospel. He's gathered a crowd of followers and already begun to annoy the Pharisees by curing the sick, teaching about forgiveness of sins, and breaking the strict sabbath rules. This is the time for him to choose the twelve apostles, and he does so after spending the night in prayer. We don't know if this was in solitude but there is a strong suggestion Jesus has taken himself off – 'He went out to the mountain' (v. 12).

Jesus has an important decision to make. Of his followers, who should become the inner circle, the closest and the most trusted? His discernment process is fully rooted in time in prayer. Is he praying for the ones he will choose, knowing how their lives will be changed? Perhaps he's praying for them to be equipped and willing to undertake the responsibilities he will give them and for them to be able to grasp the significance of the events they will witness.

'Likewise, the Spirit helps us in our weakness, for we do not know how to pray as we ought, but that very Spirit intercedes with groanings too deep for words' (Romans 8:26).

SARA BATTS-NEALE

Jesus teaches us to trust

'For everyone who asks receives, and everyone who searches finds, and for everyone who knocks, the door will be opened.' (v. 10, NRSV)

Until recently I was a trustee of a small charity that lost key grant income. We prayed for help with our finances. A year or so later, our bank balance was indeed healthier – but not because of a miraculous replacement grant. Instead, we had seen staff find new callings away from our organisation. That meant we could restructure the team and the salary costs. I'll admit this was not quite what we had in mind when we prayed for the future of the organisation but, all the same, it was the answer to our prayers.

It can be challenging when the change we see when we pray is not an obvious improvement. When we plead with God for a change – in our health, our circumstances, or our bank balance – and it doesn't arrive, it can be disheartening. Today we are taught by Jesus to trust in prayer – trust that when we ask for something, God is listening and will answer.

In my experience there is always an answer, and God does provide – just not necessarily how I was expecting! Perhaps you, like me, learned verse 9 in the simplicity of childhood and find that sits in contrast with the complexity of adult life. Maybe the key is to recognise whether we pray for our needs or our wants.

Jesus teaches us to trust – whether we are six or 60 – and to continue to make our petitions to God. One challenge for us is that the idea of the prayer these verses hint at is a transactional one. We make our requests – 'I need bread', 'I need to receive something' – and we pray in confidence to receive that exact thing. Sometimes that will happen, but for the most part, we have to trust that the outcome we see is the answer, even if it is unfathomable in the moment.

'Trust in the Lord with all your heart, and do not rely on your own insight. In all your ways acknowledge him, and he will make straight your paths' (Proverbs 3:5–6).

SARA BATTS-NEALE

Jesus teaches us to persevere

'And will not God grant justice to his chosen ones who cry to him day and night?' (v. 7, NRSV)

When I was in my 30s, I lived in London, quite near a pub called The Perseverance. I liked the pub – it was friendly and quiet – but I also loved the idea that I could find perseverance when I needed it. I was then far more impatient than the current version of me, several decades later.

Today, we are left in no doubt about the purpose of this part of Jesus' teaching. Luke tells us it is a parable about the disciples' need 'to pray always and not to lose heart' (v. 1). We thought about trust in prayer yesterday, and today we are thinking about a related idea – perseverance. Continuing in something and not losing heart is probably quite a good definition of perseverance – we just keep going, keep trusting, keep loving, keep on keeping on.

In the letter to the Romans, Paul suggests that perseverance comes from suffering and produces hope (Romans 5:3–5). Hope is the thing that, in turn, can help us persevere in prayer. Jesus talks of justice here – that persistence in prayer will lead to justice being done – 'Will he delay long in helping them?' (v. 7, NRSV). I'm puzzled about this idea that God would deliberately wait, but I am reminded of Jesus' delay in reaching Lazarus in John 11. That interval meant Jesus could fully demonstrate his power over death in the raising of Lazarus. So, we trust that God's apparent lag in showing justice is for a greater purpose – one that we cannot comprehend now but will make clear sense in the future. How far away that future is, we don't know. It is that uncertainty that makes Jesus' teaching about perseverance all the more pertinent. Jesus teaches us to persevere, to hope, and to continue in prayer.

'He has told you, O mortal, what is good, and what does the Lord require of you but to do justice and to love kindness and to walk humbly with your God?' (Micah 6:8).

SARA BATTS-NEALE

Jesus teaches us how to pray

'But whenever you pray, go into your room and shut the door and pray to your Father who is in secret.' (v. 6, NRSV)

I used to really dislike praying out loud. Even relatively recently – after I was ordained – I was asked to say grace at a relative's celebration meal. I spent a long time writing the perfect prayer because my default grace is 'Thank you, God, for dinner', which I admit might be a little too far in the direction of 'empty phrases' (v. 7), even if it is the absolute essence of giving thanks.

I have experienced some prayer meetings where every detail of every petition is brought to God. Prayer times like that can feel more like a public gossip session or a competition to see who can give God the most detail about a medical complaint. I'm pretty sure God already knows what's going on!

In our passage today we switch focus from the 'why' or the 'what' of prayer to the 'how' – Jesus tells us clearly that we do not need to use flowery phrases or to pray loudly, publicly, and obviously to be heard by God. And that's very reassuring for those of us who prefer to pray quietly. He doesn't say that other kinds of prayers aren't heard, of course.

We'll come back to the next part of Matthew 6 next week, when we look in depth at the prayer Jesus is about to teach his disciples. Today's teaching helps us understand why the prayer is relatively short. Jesus is teaching us that more is not better, that performative piety is not holy, and that private prayers are heard as much as public pronouncements. Jesus also teaches us that we should pray even though our Father already knows what we need. (Note it's what we need, not what we want, just like we thought about on Tuesday.)

'The first thing I want you to do is pray. Pray every way you know how, for everyone you know' (1 Timothy 2:1, MSG).

SARA BATTS-NEALE

Jesus teaches us where to pray

Very early in the morning, while it was still dark, Jesus got up, left the house and went off to a solitary place, where he prayed. (v. 35, NIV)

These few verses from Mark's gospel give a sense of the busyness and crowdedness of Jesus' life. Besieged by the whole town, he is unable to go openly into any other place, as his fame as a healer is spreading. It is easy to imagine Jesus – human as well as divine – being very tired and peopled-out. Jesus has taught us the 'how', the 'why', and the 'when' of prayer, and now we have a sense of the 'where'. He goes off to solitary places to pray as a counter to the busyness of his life.

Where do you pray? Do you have a particular place where you find it easy to stop and focus or are you mostly praying on the run? I remember, as a new Christian, asking a friend if I could pray on the London Underground. Yes, God hears me even if my prayer is subterranean and silent, crammed into a train with my face in someone's armpit! I longed for space and quiet in those times.

Jesus teaches us to find a space that facilitates prayer. Silence and stillness are helpful to some and an absolute nightmare to others. Lonely places are not for everyone! The idea of a silent retreat could fill you with hope and excitement or dread to the bottom of your shoes.

I wonder what happens if we deliberately try a new or different way of praying. If silence is your thing, what can you find in music or crowds? And if extrovert prayer is your preference, what happens if you are silent and still? By trying something different – and giving it a fair go – we are opening ourselves to new ways of listening to God.

God says, 'Be still, and know that I am God; I will be exalted among the nations, I will be exalted in the earth' (Psalm 46:10).

SARA BATTS-NEALE

Jesus prays in suffering

Then he returned to his disciples and found them sleeping. 'Simon,' he said to Peter, 'are you asleep? Couldn't you keep watch for one hour?' (v. 37, NIV)

We began this week thinking about Jesus praying at his baptism. Now we are listening in on him as he prays in the last hours of his life before his death on the cross. This is not pretty prayer or eloquent – this is Jesus knowing what is to come and asking to be spared it – then perhaps changing his mind, relating his coming death back to the will of the Father. It is very much a prayer that follows Jesus' own advice to keep it short, as we noticed on Thursday.

Jesus teaches us that prayer is a legitimate response to agitation and distress. I suspect I would struggle to be so resigned in the face of coming pain; I might be more fervent in my prayers for release. I do find it incredibly easy to identify with Simon Peter, who falls asleep – many are the times I've decided that I will still myself and sit quietly with the Lord only to wake up some time later.

In my church tradition there is a Maundy Thursday Watch until midnight where we pray in silence and darkness. I do find it a challenge to stay awake – a challenge, but a precious time in which to pray with Christ in these moments.

Jesus prayed at his baptism and the start of his ministry, and he prays in the final few hours before his death. Jesus teaches us to pray so that prayer runs as a tapestry thread throughout our lives. We pray in joy and sorrow, from hope in perseverance, in secret silence or in public. He teaches us to pray in love and in trust, and he teaches us that prayer is essential.

'Answer me when I call to you, my righteous God. Give me relief from my distress; have mercy on me and hear my prayer' (Psalm 4:1).

SARA BATTS-NEALE

Our Father in heaven

'This, then, is how you should pray.' (v. 9, NIV)

Last week we took Jesus' prayer habits as the basis of his teaching. This week, we will focus on the prayer he taught us. We start with Matthew's account of the prayer. In this gospel account, Jesus teaches this to the disciples as part of the longer section of the sermon on the mount, all about how we should live and pray – as we discussed on Thursday last week.

Jesus teaches us that we can call God 'our Father'. It's not just a one-to-one relationship we have with God. We have relationships with all those who also call him Father – our siblings in Christ. Faith puts us in a community and, as with our family, we don't get to choose who our brothers and sisters are. God is not more of a Father to some than to others. We are all his children. We are all one with Christ Jesus (Galatians 3:26). Jesus' prayer is the prayer of the Christian family.

The fourth-century writer Cyril of Jerusalem reckoned that because we bear the image of God, we could call ourselves 'heavens' – we are where God indwells. He developed that thought from 2 Corinthians 6:16 – 'We are the temple of the living God.' I rather like this idea as it collapses the distance between earth and heaven; we are not thinking just about how we relate to God, but also what it is to be made in and bear the image of God. Remembering this about ourselves can help us cement our understanding of our value.

So today, Jesus teaches us that we too can approach God in prayer and that we are made in the image of that God.

'In the same way, let your light shine before others, that they may see your good deeds and glorify your Father in heaven' (Matthew 5:16, NIV).

SARA BATTS-NEALE

Hallowed be your name

One day Jesus was praying in a certain place. When he finished, one of his disciples said to him, 'Lord, teach us to pray, just as John taught his disciples.' (v. 1, NIV)

Today we focus on Luke's version of the Lord's Prayer, which despite his emphasis on prayer throughout the gospel, is shorter than Matthew's. It's also interesting that in his account, Luke tells us that the disciples asked to be taught how to pray; there's no such question in Matthew. Why do you think that might be?

Luke also begins straightaway with the hallowing of God's name. Jesus teaches us to hold God's name as holy. It's not that God's name isn't already holy – we don't have to claim holiness for it every time we pray, as if the glory would slip a bit if we weren't consistent in our prayer! It's more that God's name is so frequently and easily profaned – 'Oh my God', being seen by many as quite a mild exclamation of annoyance compared to the kinds of language that's deemed acceptable for broadcast now. It is a far cry from the people of Moses' time, who did not say the name of God directly at all.

The familiarity of the Lord's Prayer can also be a bit of a stumbling block. We sometimes need a reminder of the need for awe and reverence in our dealings with the creator of the universe. Hallowing God's name is another way we are prompted to ensure we have not made God too small or have become too casual in our prayers.

Jesus teaches us to remember who God is when we address God in our prayers – and by extension, when we pray to Jesus or the Holy Spirit, to offer due reverence to those persons of the Trinity, too.

'You shall not make wrongful use of the name of the Lord your God, for the Lord will not acquit anyone who misuses his name' (Exodus 20:7, NRSV).

SARA BATTS-NEALE

Your kingdom come

'Truly I tell you, anyone who will not receive the kingdom of God like a little child will never enter it.' (v. 15, NIV)

Do you know the Taizé chant which tells us the kingdom of God is justice and peace? In the gospel there are many parables to explain the kingdom – mustard seeds, yeast, fishing nets, buried treasure – all giving us a sense of growth that might look ordinary but is in fact rather special. I think of an old, crackly, untuned radio – every now and then we pick up a signal that is clear and coherent but most of the time it's just static. In the same way, every now and then a kingdom moment clearly breaks through into ordinary life: reconciliation happens; injustice is avoided; love prevails over hate. In God's kingdom, love, justice, and mercy prevail. God's values, not our small, petty, human values triumph.

The kingdom values are very different from ours. Today's passage gives an example of this. The disciples seem to be working on society's values and so want to keep the troublesome toddlers from the teacher. They're rebuked by Jesus, who turns those values upside down. The children are the ones who will understand.

So when Jesus teaches us to pray for the kingdom to come, we are praying for a just, loving, and merciful society to prevail. It's an amazing shorthand for holding before God so many of the places in the world where these values are absent. As I write, for instance, there is a real fear that far-right political parties will continue to gain power and usher in a new era where love for all God's people is far down the agenda. When we pray for the kingdom to come, we are praying that we will see the kingdom moments more clearly. Jesus is teaching us to find ways in our own lives and communities to encourage the green shoots of his kingdom to break through.

'Therefore, since we are receiving a kingdom that cannot be shaken, let us be thankful, and so worship God acceptably with reverence and awe' (Hebrews 12:28).

SARA BATTS-NEALE

Your will be done on earth as it is in heaven

And the world and its desire are passing away, but those who do the will of God abide forever. (v. 17, NRSV)

The poem by Teresa of Ávila that begins 'Christ has no body but yours...' really resonated with my sense of calling to ministry. We think about the body of Christ more often in terms of Paul's description – different people building up a community (1 Corinthians 12) – so it's interesting to think about us being literally the body of Christ.

Jesus teaches us to long for the will of God to be done. My sense, informed by Teresa of Ávila, is that we're not just praying for constant miraculous intervention but also that we are the instruments by which God's will is done. Cyril of Jerusalem, who we met on Sunday, reckoned that in heaven, the angels carried out God's will. On earth, it's us.

Today we read a passage from 1 John which reminds us of the fleeting values of a life lived not by God's will but by the standards of the world. Few of us will lead the kind of life that has a national or international impact, but we all can choose to align ourselves with God's will – not necessarily searching for the one 'right' way to be, but working towards the kingdom values of love, mercy, and justice that we discussed yesterday. Love is the starting point for living that life. It's the everyday choices we make that cumulatively can change a life – ours, someone else's, or the way a community thinks.

Verses 12–14 also carry an echo of the whole Lord's Prayer – knowing the Father, forgiveness of sins, vanquishing evil – helping us to see how this idea of God's will being done sits at the heart of a changed life. We love others because that's God's will for us. Everything else is a diversion.

'And looking at those who sat around him, he said, "Here are my mother and my brothers! Whoever does the will of God is my brother and sister and mother"' (Mark 3:34–35).

SARA BATTS-NEALE

Give us this day our daily bread

'At twilight you shall eat meat, and in the morning you shall have your fill of bread; then you shall know that I am the Lord your God.' (v. 12, NRSV)

Wholemeal or white? Wheat flour or spelt? What kind of bread do you prefer? It's got to be wholemeal with bits in for me, and there's got to be proper butter if I'm making toast. Bread is still a staple food despite the wide changes in our diets in my lifetime. Where would a packed lunch be without the stalwart cheese sandwich – although rather than the white sliced and mild cheddar of my childhood, there are hundreds of combinations of breads and cheese on offer nowadays.

What bread is it that we're asking for today? We have two things to think about. Jesus is teaching us that we need just enough, like the Israelites gathering manna. We are called to a radical trust that if we ask, God will provide, just as we thought about last week. Having just enough goes against everything our consumer society encourages – you don't get your daily bread on a bulk-buy 'buy one get one free'. Remember what happened when the Israelites tried to gather more manna than they needed for each day? It spoiled.

The second thought today's line sparks is that of bread as a staple for our physical life. Jesus says, 'I am the bread of life' (John 6:35); that is, he is the staple for our spiritual life. Jesus is essential. For some of us, we will see this essentialness reflected in our Eucharist – we receive the bread of life at the communion rail. Your church practice may differ, and so the emphasis is on the metaphor instead. Either way, this part of the Lord's Prayer profoundly emphasises our dependence on, and need of, Jesus. Jesus teaches us to trust that our daily needs will be met and reminds us that our spiritual well-being relies upon him.

'I am the living bread that came down from heaven. Whoever eats of this bread will live forever, and the bread that I will give for the life of the world is my flesh' (John 6:51).

SARA BATTS-NEALE

Forgive us our trespasses

Then Peter came to Jesus and asked, 'Lord, how many times shall I forgive my brother or sister who sins against me? Up to seven times?' (v. 21, NIV)

Do you trespass or sin? Jesus teaches us to be alert to our own forgiveness when we relate to those who wound us. In our culture, sin is often trivialised and portrayed as only being about the body – we eat something 'naughty', as if foodstuffs had an inherent moral value, for example.

'Trespass' conveys the idea of being in a place we shouldn't be, infringing on another's person or property. Sin therefore isn't just about my own body, but how I treat other people. Am I recognising the image of God in someone else, as I would want the image of God in me to be recognised? And if I am recognising the image of God in someone else, am I truly forgiving them as God has forgiven me?

Jesus teaches us to forgive and to recognise our own forgiven-ness. Forgiveness is not the same as saying that hurts don't matter – that somehow forgiveness minimises what's happened. That's not the case. Forgiveness is saying that the person matters more than the offence. Restitution is a good thing, but forgiveness is not contingent on it. If you owe me cash, and I forgive the debt, I value you more than the money. I demonstrate my love for you, but I am still out of pocket. Forgiveness does not remove the consequences of our actions.

It's hard when we are hurt by others to contemplate offering forgiveness – is it akin to us backing down? When we remember that we are infinitely forgiven by our loving God, it becomes easier. But it takes practice, patience, and love – Jesus tells Simon Peter to forgive not seven times, but seventy times seven. Seventy is not just a concrete number but a representation of completeness, so Jesus teaches that our forgiveness should be unlimited.

'Then he took a cup, and after giving thanks he gave it to them, saying, "Drink from it, all of you, for this is my blood of the covenant, which is poured out for many for the forgiveness of sins"' (Matthew 26:27–28, NRSV).

SARA BATTS-NEALE

Lead us not into temptation but deliver us from evil

'My prayer is not that you take them out of the world but that you protect them from the evil one.' (v. 15, NIV)

I've loved learning to row with a local coastal rowing club. Launching a boat has seen me waist deep in the river feeling the unseen force of the tide as it tries to pull the boat away from me in a direction I don't want it to go. Perhaps that's why I like Cyril of Jerusalem's lovely image for temptation as a river we need to cross. If we are fit, we will be strong enough to resist the current and make it to the other side. If we are not fit, we will be swept away by the tide of temptation.

I like that metaphor because it relates to both the ubiquity of temptation and the need to be well prepared – wearing the spiritual equivalent of the waders I pull on before walking out into the river. This is partly what our discipleship is all about – finding good patterns of prayer and trust that help us deal with the inevitable temptations that come our way. Jesus teaches us to acknowledge the ubiquity of temptation, and he teaches us to recognise evil.

I wonder how you think about evil. There are evils out there – war, genocide, injustice to name three – and I believe in the existence of the 'evil one', who would work to knock us off our course. In today's passage from John's gospel, we eavesdrop on Jesus' wonderful final prayer. He's telling God – for our benefit – that his followers now understand the message he has shared, and he rightly gives glory to God and claims that glory for himself. Then, in verse 20, he prays for you and me because we believed through the disciples' teachings. What an amazing idea! That's a fabulous moment to end our exploration of prayer with Jesus, isn't it?

Jesus, thank you for praying for me. Thank you for your words and example that teach me how to pray. May you know my heart, and I yours, as we journey together. Amen.

SARA BATTS-NEALE

Let kindness light the way

Catherine Larner writes…

Kindness is a word, a concept, that can be seen as a bit slight, rather twee, a bit soft. In today's individualistic society, it can even be seen as a weakness to be kind to people when we are encouraged to push forward with our career or goals in life, both professionally and personally.

On the political stage or in big business, ruthless, self-serving, bullying practices seem to be the norm, and this behaviour has become a model for communities, most clearly evident in social media.

In my own circle of work, a normally accepted behaviour of politeness and respect has gradually but pervasively been lacking in people I've dealt with. It's caused me to feel dejected and demoralised, questioning my own self-worth. Then I found that it wasn't just my experience, friends and colleagues had found the same. Why had there been this change in normal everyday courtesy and kindness?

For Christians, kindness is a fruit of the Spirit. It is how we show love and compassion for others and an opportunity for our actions to shine, presenting a different and distinct motivation and mindset from that of the world. However, I can't recall hearing a sermon on the subject. Perhaps we take it for granted – we all know how to be kind, don't we?

When you have been on the receiving end of unkind words or actions, kindness is a quality which comes to matter a great deal. Many people can speak of how they have been wounded by behaviours in the workplace, in their family or wider relationships, and in the church.

Much as we should avoid hurtful words and actions, actively reaching out with kindness can bring joy and connection and peace in conflict. Acts of kindness can prove life-changing for both giver and receiver. With kindness we can actually change the world, and in these difficult times that's something worth exploring, I think. Will you join me?

Bringing light to darkness

Do not repay evil with evil or insult with insult. On the contrary, repay evil with blessing, because to this you were called so that you may inherit a blessing. (v. 9, NIV)

Why are people unkind? Is it because they want to remain in control and keep the upper hand? Or because they are lazy and don't care how their actions are received? Perhaps they have been treated unkindly and want to retaliate through someone else.

How do we feel when we experience unkindness? They say kindness is contagious and we should 'pass it on', but maybe unkindness is too.

Unkind behaviours are all around us in our communities, our nation, and our world, but if we focus solely on the conflicts, greed, and selfishness we will continue to be brought low. Instead of thinking of all that is bad and letting unkind behaviour get us down, we could seek and model good, kind words and actions. God doesn't just call us to be kind to those who are pleasant to us or when we expect something in return. Instead, we are called to show forgiveness, understanding, and compassion to everyone, just as he has done for us.

When we experience harsh words or dismissive, inconsiderate behaviour, we can think about smiling or being positive and encouraging. I tried this in my work situation and was astonished at how much it changed not only my attitude for the better, but I also received a lovely response back.

People we meet may be going through a difficult time. They may have financial or personal problems or are being bullied or pressured at work. They may be worn down by the lack of kindness they are being shown. 'Be kind,' said Plato, 'for everyone you meet is fighting a harder battle.'

If we want to see a world where kindness is the norm, we need to look for the light of kindness in others and in ourselves. And the more kindness we show, the more others may follow.

Help me, Lord, not to be cruel or angry when people aren't kind. Give me your strength to show them kindness and understanding. Amen.

CATHERINE LARNER

Radiating kindness

But the fruit of the spirit is love, joy, peace, forbearance, kindness, goodness, faithfulness, gentleness and self-control. (vv. 22–23, NIV)

Most of us would like to think we are kind. We might give to charity and perhaps hold the door open for a stranger. We might greet someone in the street, bake a neighbour a cake, or buy a friend a coffee. It could be we think of these behaviours as second nature and not worthy of comment, but in recent years, care for our neighbour has appeared lacking. People typically seem to be less generous, more aggressive, more easily offended, and less willing to listen.

We still look for kindness, though. Posts on social media showing 'random acts of kindness' attract millions of views. Television and radio programmes highlight individuals who are generous to their communities, and a survey last year found children chose 'kindness' as their word of the year.

So, what do we understand kindness to mean? It is more than simply being 'nice' and not wanting to upset people or be thought of badly. Instead, it is about being gentle, caring and helpful, selfless, compassionate, and merciful. It involves a generosity of spirit, making another person feel cared for and cherished. It is bold and courageous, not expecting anything in return. These are high aims, but we have Jesus as our example and the Holy Spirit as our helper.

While it is true that some people seem naturally to be kind, it's said that kindness is a muscle we should all be exercising. In his book *Love Kindness* (Tyndale House, 2019), Barry Corey says it should be as natural to us as breathing – exhaling kindness after we've inhaled the breath of the Holy Spirit.

As we invite God's Spirit to work in our life, let's radiate kindness, offering hope and happiness to people we meet and displaying something of the wonder of Christ.

Father, fill me anew with your Spirit today. Help me to grow the fruit of kindness in my life. Amen.

CATHERINE LARNER

Brightening someone's day

Therefore, as God's chosen people, holy and dearly loved, clothe yourself with compassion, kindness, humility, gentleness and patience. (v. 12, NIV)

Bernadette Russell challenged herself to undertake 366 days of kindness. In her book *Conversations on Kindness* (Elliott & Thompson, 2025), she remembers queuing in a post office. A young man in a hoodie turned away from the counter because he didn't have enough money for a stamp. Bernadette offered to buy it. 'He seemed completely taken aback by that tiny act of kindness… he said thanks several times and we smiled at each other.'

Learning about acts of kindness like this fills me with hope and optimism. Psychologist Jonathan Haidt says it can 'make us feel warm and tingly' and 'wipes away our cynical feelings'.

Research has found that relationships, politics, and the workplace can all be improved through kindness. The University of Sussex has a Centre for Research on Kindness and found that seemingly inconsequential gestures or comments, like a smile, a compliment, or friendliness from a stranger can bring about connection and transformation.

I remember being in a supermarket car park and spotting a woman with her trolley looking around. I caught her eye, and she gave an embarrassed laugh. 'I can't find my car,' she explained. After asking for details, I soon spotted a likely candidate. 'That's it!' she said. 'Thank you, my darling!'

I could have avoided making eye contact or just wished her well in her predicament, but those few seconds when I could help filled me with a sense of purpose and joy and a brief connection with a stranger.

Paul tells us to think about our attitude each day, to 'put on the new self' in Christ, clothing ourselves in kindness, just as if we are getting dressed spiritually as well as physically. By showing kindness, we are learning more about the nature of Christ and God's plan for his world.

Father, remind me that I am clothed in kindness today and help me to be bold, courageous, and generous in reaching out to others, showing them something of your love. Amen.

CATHERINE LARNER

It's all good

A kind-hearted woman gains honour, but ruthless men gain only wealth. Those who are kind benefit themselves, but the cruel bring ruin on themselves. (vv. 16–17, NIV)

When I think about a good boss, teacher, or nurse it's usually because they were kind, thoughtful, and caring. They saw me not as a means to an end, delivering a result or performance, but as an individual with my own skills, challenges, and triumphs.

Kindness is a quality we appreciate and admire, and researchers say it defines us as humans and is vital for good society. But it also brings psychological and emotional benefits to us as people.

We feel happy when we are kind to others and when someone is kind to us. We even feel happy if we see or think of someone else being kind! Experiencing kindness in any way can lift our spirits and increase our self-esteem and optimism.

Scientists have identified hormones which are released when we perform acts of kindness, and these improve our moods and mental health, lower our blood pressure, and lessen our likelihood of diabetes. Kindness can reduce loneliness and strengthen communities, and it achieves ripples of happiness as acts of kindness initiate other acts of kindness.

The 'pay it forward' movement has long been an example of a means of showing generosity to strangers. There are lots of places where you can leave money behind the counter for the next person to receive a free cup of coffee or a book. But increasingly I've heard of people who've bought a stranger's shopping or petrol because they haven't enough money. Instead of arranging to be reimbursed, they've said 'pay it forward' so someone else will benefit from an act of kindness. It's incredibly powerful.

Kindness begins by thinking of others more than ourselves and looking outside of our own concerns. We never regret showing kindness. It blesses both the one who receives and the one who gives. It always makes a difference.

Father, show me ways in which you'd like me to reach out to others with kindness today. Amen.

CATHERINE LARNER

A change of heart

'But to you who are listening I say: love your enemies, do good to those who hate you, bless those who curse you, pray for those who ill-treat you.' (vv. 27–28, NIV)

It's easy to be kind to people we know will receive us warmly, but how do we feel about reaching out to people who have wronged us?

It can be difficult to be kind if someone's been cruel or malicious towards us or if we bear a grudge. But we are told to forgive, and if we are following God's example, we should be willing to make the first move and offer peace and love to others. The poet Robert Burns said that the kind heart most resembles God. I've found that when I retaliate to unpleasantness, I feel badly towards both myself and the other person, and the situation can escalate.

These days, we're seeing leaders who delight in their lawlessness, their disdain for the poor, and their lack of mercy for the dispossessed and vulnerable. However, in a review of the band Peace, for the London Institute for Contemporary Christianity, Josh Hinton said: 'True power, true freedom, is found in the simple rebellion of being kind'. He had recently discovered the band's album *Kindness Is the New Rock and Roll* and found it to be hugely significant.

Jesus' mission wasn't to run roughshod over the unscrupulous and selfish, Josh continued: 'His people wanted a political-military leader to give them victory. They didn't get one. Likewise, if we find ourselves smiling when selfish leaders punch down, perhaps we need reminding – kindness is the true rock and roll.'

Whereas condemnation and judgement can bring stubbornness and rebellion, kindness can lead to repentance and a change of heart. We can see that it deflects conflict and confrontation, bringing peace and reconciliation. So we need someone to take the first step of kindness. Perhaps that needs to be me today.

Soften my heart, Lord, to be sensitive to the needs of others and give me courage and boldness to reach out to them. Amen.

CATHERINE LARNER

Modelling behaviour

Be kind and compassionate to one another, forgiving each other, just as in Christ God forgave you. (v. 32, NIV)

These days, posts on social media seem not only to reflect behaviour but also to direct it. This is damaging, as we are aware, but there are instances where it can also be positive and uplifting. Increasingly, it is where we see examples of good and kind acts. Someone might film themselves giving flowers to strangers in the street or thrusting a wad of notes at someone who's clearly going through a tough time.

Making these gestures so public may appear wrong, but researchers say we are more likely to do something if we see others doing it. If more people act kindly towards each other, we will inevitably see a kinder society. So social media can help us in making creative, inventive acts of kindness widespread.

However, we don't need 'influencers' to model kindness, for the Bible is our ultimate guide, and there are dozens of verses about kindness in both the Old and New Testaments. Stories like Rahab, Ruth and Naomi, and David and Jonathan, and words of wisdom, instruction, and encouragement in the Psalms, Proverbs, and Paul's letters.

Above all we have the embodiment of kindness through Jesus. He touched the sick, spent time with the lonely, and had dinner with social outcasts. He wasn't racist or sexist. He didn't overlook people who were disabled or refugees. He spent time with the woman at the well who had been ostracised (John 4), he got alongside the man with leprosy who was feared and shunned (Matthew 8), and he even forgave those who hurt and betrayed him (Luke 23).

Jesus didn't perform random acts of kindness to make himself feel good. He had a deeper purpose to reveal who God is and the extent of his love for the world, that we might share and experience it.

Thank you, Lord, for all the love and kindness you have shown. Please work through me that I might bring more of your kindness to the people I meet today. Amen.

CATHERINE LARNER

Kind words

Let a righteous man strike me – that is a kindness; let him rebuke me – that is oil on my head. (v. 5, NIV)

Kindness doesn't always mean bringing light and joy into a situation, and it isn't necessarily the easiest option. Jesus challenged the social norms of the time and spoke with courage and conviction, though still with a quiet, gentle, composed authority.

Today there seems to be a difficulty in handling opposing points of view or disagreeing courteously and respectfully. Politicians mock and bay at each other. Leaders often ridicule and belittle to assert their authority. Differences of opinion are shouted down in work meetings and social settings, and there's little nuance of debate on social media.

All too many situations seem to be polarised into right and wrong, black and white, yet issues are more complex than ever. People will always have different opinions and beliefs, but we can learn to debate, discuss, and argue with grace, gentleness, and consideration for each other.

We can still show kindness even when there are difficult things to say. There may be times when we keep someone accountable or point out a misunderstanding or an error. It's important, then, to speak boldly and plainly. Equally, there are times when we might have to receive this too and then apologise to the person we have wronged, and to the Lord, and seek to do better next time. Kind words are ones which keep us on the path to righteousness.

I realised I could be critical of others, but I saw people differently when I was going through a difficult time, because of the kindness they showed me. I went on to learn that instead of seeing what I perceived as wrong in others, I needed to be mindful of the kindness of the Lord and to see people as he sees them. Kindness breaks down barriers, heals the hurts, and binds us together.

Lord, thank you for your example. Please teach me courage and discernment today, to know when to speak out and when to not, and to bring kindness to all the situations I meet. Amen.

CATHERINE LARNER

Good intentions

And what does the Lord require of you? To act justly and to love mercy and to walk humbly with your God. (v. 8, NIV)

During the Covid pandemic people seemed not only willing but also eager to show kindness to others. Various initiatives have arisen at different times to counter cruel or tragic events over the years, like #BeKind or 'pay it forward'. We've seen communities come together in extreme weather events or to restore property after riots. Sadly, the momentum of these initiatives does diminish, but genuine, heartfelt kindness is a powerful force and something we can nurture day by day.

In these difficult times, when I feel powerless in bringing about change, I remember that kindness is a gift with which we are all equipped. Each day we can think about the people we'll meet and where we'll be. Can we send someone a card or a text or invite someone round for a meal?

I have a lovely friend who, if she hears someone is having a hard time, will put a card and chocolate buttons through their door or a bunch of flowers on the doorstep. And she always has a spare umbrella in her car so if someone's caught in the rain, she'll stop and give them the umbrella.

'I have found that it is the small everyday deeds of ordinary folks that keep the darkness at bay,' J.R.R. Tolkien wrote in *The Hobbit*. 'Small acts of kindness and love.'

If we genuinely seek to follow Jesus' example in how we live our lives, then surely we would seek to show loving kindness to everyone, with no attention to ourselves and seeking no reward.

We will never feel bad by being kind, and no act of kindness, no matter how small, is ever wasted. We have no idea how much our acts of kindness can impact others. Let's reach out with kindness today.

Father, please work through my small acts of kindness today, bringing your joy, love, and mercy to the people I meet and the situations I face. Amen.

CATHERINE LARNER

Because he first loved us

But when the kindness and love of God our Saviour appeared, he saved us, not because of righteous things we had done, but because of his mercy. (vv. 4–5, NIV)

We shouldn't forget that we were first shown kindness by God. We were sinners, facing death, and he extended love and grace, giving his Son to die for us. The kindness of God is the key to our salvation, and it's vast. In gratitude, and to present something of God to others, we should be loving, merciful, and forgiving.

It's something the early Christians were known for. The word Christian is closely associated with the Greek word for kindness, *chrestotes*, so they became known as 'the kind ones'. Certainly, as we seek to be salt and light in our world and share the gospel, we should be mindful of how we are caring for our neighbours.

I find the words of William Booth, founder of the Salvation Army, very powerful: 'You cannot warm the hearts of people with God's love if they have an empty stomach and cold feet.' I'm also moved by stories of people who give freely of their skills and time, like London hairdresser Joshua Coombes who cuts the hair of homeless people. His care and attention, treating them as individuals, made them feel better about themselves and reduced their sense of isolation. He started the #DoSomethingForNothing initiative.

One of my favourite Bible passages is Hebrews 13:1–2, where we are encouraged to entertain strangers because they might be angels in disguise. Isn't that a challenge? However, whether or not they are angels or wounded, fallible beings like ourselves, we are urged to reach out. Kindness brings joy and positivity in our lives, and it can change the world around us, too.

Simple acts of kindness or selfless behaviour stand out like beacons in a dark, difficult world, reassuring us of our common humanity and the hope we have in a greater good. Let's shine with kindness today.

Father God, help me to picture and embody a kinder culture, a new way of living today. Give me your heart for people, to show forgiveness, compassion, and love. Amen.

CATHERINE LARNER

Bearing fruit

'Remain in me, as I also remain in you. No branch can bear fruit by itself; it must remain in the vine. Neither can you bear fruit unless you remain in me.'
JOHN 15:4 (NIV)

As a charity, BRF Ministries is always doing a huge assortment of things, from our Anna Chaplaincy team equipping people to minister to older people to our Messy Church team bringing Jesus to families across the world. From our Parenting for Faith ministry reaching parents and church leaders to transform ideas about how to raise God-connected children to our BRF Resources, which span so many different topics to help people to develop their faith journey.

At a glance these activities might seem distant or disparate, but a closer look shows the vine from which all our ministries grow – the mission set out by Leslie Mannering over 100 years ago, to which we still hold today: inspiring people of all ages to grow in Christian faith. God is at the heart of all that we do, and we are hugely thankful for all the fruit we have born through these works over the last century and more.

We want to keep building on this work, adapting, growing and finding even more glorious ways for people to grow in their faith while still remaining rooted to our mission.

This work would not be possible without kind donations from individuals, charitable trusts and gifts in wills. If you would like to support us now and in the future, you can become a Friend of BRF Ministries by making a monthly gift of £2 or more. We thank you for your friendship.

Find out more at **brf.org.uk/donate** or get in touch with us on **+44 (0)1865 319700** or via **giving@brf.org.uk**.

We thank you for your support and your prayers.

The fundraising team at BRF Ministries

Give. Pray. Get involved.
brf.org.uk

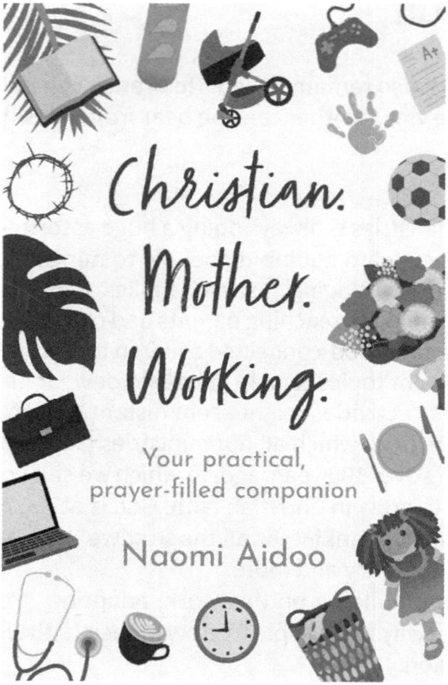

Christian. Mother. Working – in that order. It's easy to look at life only through the lens of being a Christian mum. But could we weave our other important work into the equation? In *Christian. Mother. Working.* Naomi Aidoo considers how family and faith impact our work in each of life's seasons. With more and more mothers in the workforce, she shows how working motherhood is something to be celebrated as we display our gifts and the call on our lives in areas which extend beyond our families, offering prayerful, practical prompts to encourage flourishing and fulfilment.

Christian. Mother. Working.
Your practical, prayer-filled companion
Naomi Aidoo
978 1 80039 438 4   £9.99
brfresources.org.uk

In *Come for Refuge*, Pete Wilcox, bishop of Sheffield, invites you to read the book of Ruth through the lens of the present global migration crisis. By interweaving an exposition of the text of Ruth with testimonies from contemporary migrants, creating a conversation between the two, this book offers a hopeful vision of what migration can contribute to the world.

Come for Refuge
The book of Ruth and hope for migrants
Pete Wilcox
978 1 80039 549 7 £9.99
brfresources.org.uk

To order

Online: **brfresources.org.uk**
Telephone: **+44 (0)1865 319700**
Mon–Fri 9.30–17.00

Delivery times within the UK are normally 15 working days. Prices are correct at the time of going to press but may change without prior notice.

BRF

Title	Price	Qty	Total
Day by Day with God (May–Aug 2026) – single copy	£5.99		
Day by Day with God (Sep–Dec 2026) – single copy	£5.99		
Christian. Mother. Working.	£9.99		
Come for Refuge	£9.99		

POSTAGE AND PACKING CHARGES			
Order value	UK	Europe	Rest of world
Under £7.00	£2.00	Available on request	Available on request
£7.00–£29.99	£3.00		
£30.00 and over	FREE		

Total value of books	
Donation	
Postage and packing	
Total for this order	

Please complete in BLOCK CAPITALS

Title ________ First name/initials ________________ Surname ______________________________

Address ____

____ Postcode ______________

Acc. No. ______________________ Telephone ______________________________

Email ____

Method of payment

❑ Cheque (made payable to BRF) ❑ MasterCard / Visa

Card no. ☐☐☐☐ ☐☐☐☐ ☐☐☐☐ ☐☐☐☐

Expires end M M Y Y

BRF Ministries Gift Aid Declaration

giftaid it

In order to Gift Aid your donations, you must tick the box below.

❑ I want to Gift Aid my donation and any donation I make in the future or have made in the past four years to BRF Ministries.

I am a UK taxpayer and understand that if I pay less Income Tax and/or Capital Gains Tax in the current tax year than the amount of Gift Aid claimed on all my donations, it is my responsibility to pay any difference. Please notify BRF Ministries if you want to cancel this declaration, change your name or home address, or no longer pay sufficient tax on your income and/or capital gains.

We will use your personal data to process this order. From time to time we may send you information about the work of BRF Ministries. Please contact us if you wish to discuss your mailing preferences. Our privacy policy is available at **brf.org.uk/privacy.**

Please return this form to:

BRF Ministries, 15 The Chambers, Vineyard, Abingdon OX14 3FE

For terms and cancellation information, please visit **brfresources.org.uk/terms**

Registered with FUNDRAISING REGULATOR

DAY BY DAY WITH GOD INDIVIDUAL SUBSCRIPTION FORM

To set up a recurring subscription, please go to
brfresources.org.uk/subscriptions

Please note our new subscription rates, current until 30 April 2027:

Individual subscriptions
covering 3 issues for under 6 copies, payable in advance (including postage & packing):

	UK	Europe	Rest of world
Day by Day with God	£25.20	£37.50	£44.25

Copies may also be obtained from Christian bookshops at £5.99 per copy.

Title ___________ First name/initials _______________ Surname ____________________________________

Address ____

____ Postcode ________________________

Telephone _____________________________ Email ____

Please send ***Day by Day with God*** beginning with the September 2026 / January 2027 / May 2027 issue (*delete as appropriate*):

(*please tick box*)	UK	Europe	Rest of world
1-year subscription	☐ £25.20	☐ £37.50	☐ £44.25

Optional donation to support the work of BRF Ministries £ ___________________

Total enclosed £ ___________________ (cheques should be made payable to 'BRF')

Please complete and return the Gift Aid declaration on p. 142 to make your donation even more valuable to us.

Please charge my MasterCard / Visa with £ _________________

Card no. ☐☐☐☐ ☐☐☐☐ ☐☐☐☐ ☐☐☐☐

Expires end M M Y Y

We will use your personal data to process this order. From time to time we may send you information about the work of BRF Ministries. Please contact us if you wish to discuss your mailing preferences. Our privacy policy is available at **brf.org.uk/privacy.**

Please return this form to:

BRF Ministries, 15 The Chambers, Vineyard, Abingdon OX14 3FE
For terms and cancellation information, please visit **brfresources.org.uk/terms**.